Since its founding in 1970, the Community College of Vermont (CCV) has been dedicated to a mission of providing students access to college statewide. In a state with only 500,000 people, the college built a delivery model that leverages the resources of the communities it serves. As a result, CCV has been successful in bringing high-quality postsecondary education to within 25 miles of 95% of the state's population. For 34 years, all CCV instruction has been delivered with part-time faculty. For decades, this characteristic was an anomaly in higher education. To defend against the inevitable criticism, CCV became very skilled at developing and supporting part-time faculty. As the use of part-time faculty has increased throughout higher education, other colleges have approached CCV in order to learn from our experience how to ensure quality instruction with part-time faculty.

In 1992, CCV developed its first "teaching for development" handbook. At the 2003 annual convention of the American Association of Community Colleges, we introduced a major revision of the handbook as part of a presentation titled "Supporting Adjunct Faculty and Instructors as if Your Life Depended on It." As a result of the overwhelming response to that presentation and the handbook, we embarked on a project to rewrite the handbook for a wider audience, resulting in the text you have in front of you.

This guide combines both theory and practice and focuses on the role of faculty in engaging students, celebrating learning, and developing students' skills. Learning is a collective enterprise—ongoing, always unfinished, exciting, transformational—as much for instructors and staff as for students. The guide attempts to capture that spirit of learning in its approach to teaching, providing guidelines and suggestions that have proven effective in the classroom. In addition, there are opportunities here for instructors to reflect on their values and goals.

The book is divided into four sections. Part 1 provides an overview of community college history and tradition, including commonalities in values, curricular scope, and student-centered focus. Part 2 explores community college students, their diversity, and their development. In Part 3, teaching strategies are aligned with the structure of the semester, providing instructors with ideas for creating syllabi, organizing content, using small groups, responding to student crises, and much more. Part 4 presents different teaching methods and classroom management guidelines, explores how instructors can develop students' academic skills, and describes best practices for giving and receiving feedback.

Throughout this guide you will find specific strategies for teaching—the kind of practical advice that circulates among veteran teachers whenever they gather together—but you will also find an emphasis on the spirit of teaching and learning, the reflective aspects that deepen our understanding of and appreciation for the tremendous work that happens regularly in the community college classroom.

This edition has been written by Deborah A. Stewart, whom you will recognize as a gifted writer and teacher. Deborah's journey with CCV began as an adult student who graduated in 1989 and continued her education to earn a bachelor's degree and a master's of fine arts in poetry. She returned to CCV in 1993 as a part-time instructor and joined the CCV staff in 1997 as an academic coordinator. Deborah is currently an associate academic dean at CCV.

This guide is a product of many hands and minds:

- Dick Eisele, who wrote CCV's first handbook, *Teaching for Development: A Handbook for Instructors*, and remains a teaching inspiration for many. Others, too numerous to be listed, contributed to that first edition and those that followed.

■ People who reviewed and offered feedback on this revised and expanded edition. Thanks in particular to Jen Alberico, David Buchdahl, Natalie Searle, Dee Steffan, and Rebecca Werner.

■ The CCV community at large—instructors, staff, and students—who, over the years, have so generously shared their lessons, their enthusiasm, and their insights in order to enrich teaching and learning for all.

■ Community colleges whose commitment to mission we admire—some of whom are cited in this publication.

■ A special thank you is in order to Dr. George Boggs and AACC. His curiosity about CCV's anomaly of having 100% part-time faculty quickly became an interest in how increasingly important development of part-time faculty is to every community college. At his urging, we began our wonderful collaboration with Deanna D'Errico of the Community College Press.

Timothy J. Donovan
President
Community College of Vermont

Why Teach at a Community College?

My own reasons for teaching are relatively straightforward. I was a community college student; not only did I benefit from the experience, but also my life has been altogether shaped by it. As an adolescent, I dreamed of furthering my education. Despite moving numerous times in junior and senior high school, I had a record of good grades and the support of a few special teachers. However, I also faced some significant challenges. I was the child of a single parent, and no one in my family had attended college or understood what the process entailed. In addition to being unable to afford tuition, my family was deeply distrustful of the programs that claimed to assist needy students.

My mother worried that, among other things, I would be stranded at a college campus with no money to take classes and no money to come home. These kinds of fears, real or imagined, led her to envision education less as an opportunity than a risk. In the process, I developed my own set of doubts. I feared that good grades were not enough, that somehow, as my mother predicted, I would find myself marooned in a world I was ill-equipped to navigate—and not just financially, but also socially and culturally. I did not just wonder whether I could succeed; I wondered whether I would belong.

As a result, I delayed college for several years, concentrating instead on working, getting married, and having children. All the time, my determination grew. When I finally enrolled, I chose a college in my local community. I will not say my fears disappeared. Like many of the students I have come to know over the years, I feared I would not succeed, that I did not deserve to succeed, and I anguished over what succeeding would mean to those who were closest to me. First-generation college students often have such concerns, because pursuing an education—a different way of life— can mean separation from the very sources of support in their lives.

These fears can be alleviated in part if students establish new sources of support and modeling and find ways to bridge their old and new lives. Certainly, this was true for me, and in most cases, these models came from the classroom, from my instructors. Not only did they act as ambassadors, welcoming me into their respective learning communities, but these instructors also encouraged me in my own faltering attempts to understand, to speak, and to know. I am not sure if even they realized how tentatively I considered myself a college student. Of course, over time and with successes, I built enough confidence and strength to take on a baccalaureate and a graduate program. It all began, however, with the dedicated community college teachers who simultaneously encouraged and challenged me.

I do not know how many instructors began as I did, a student in the very community college where I now work. However, students are still the reason so many choose to teach in this setting. In community colleges, teaching is the instructor's primary responsibility, and although this often means less emphasis on research, it also means more opportunity to develop one's expertise in the classroom. Students are richly diverse, representing the wide range of individuals you would meet in society itself, and they enter the classroom with varying levels of academic preparedness. Although teaching has its challenges, it also brings significant rewards. If I learned much as a student, I have learned even more as a teacher. Students have not only offered me fresh insight and nuances into the subjects I love, they have taught me about myself as a person.

Last year, at the college where I work and teach, we asked instructors their reasons for teaching there. They responded overwhelmingly that it was because of students. Instructor after instructor recounted stories about a moment in which they had connected with a student, the flash of understanding on a student's face, and the feeling of having made a difference, even a small one, in someone's life. They wrote about students who inspired them to be the best kinds of teachers, ones who teach with passion and empathy, who feel bolstered in even the most difficult circumstances by their students' trust.

Just as the students at our college are fairly representative of all community college students, so, too, do our instructors share much with their peers elsewhere. According to Cohen and Brawer (2003), community college teachers in general are more satisfied than are university faculty with regard to pay, institutional and departmental reputation, time spent with their families, and collegial relationships with other faculty. This does not mean that community college instructors do not wish for more development opportunities for themselves and better motivated and prepared students: They do (Cohen & Brawer, 2003).

And although it may be difficult, from an instructor's perspective, to increase a student's preparedness for the classroom, there are many things that colleges are doing to address this concern, including early assessment of skills, developmental opportunities, freshman seminar courses, and other institutional supports for students. In addition, there are things we can do as instructors to make the very most of our learning environments. First and foremost, perhaps, we can develop ourselves as teachers through the sharing of ideas with other faculty and reflecting deeply on the choices we make in the classroom. It is important for all teachers to feel supported and nurtured in their work.

That is the primary reason for this guide. I hope new and veteran teachers will find information here to enhance their teaching experience, and, in the process, enhance the experience of learners. Obviously, a handbook can only skim the surface of most topics, but it can whet an instructor's appetite for learning more and for talking with other teachers. If this book accomplishes that, I will be delighted.

Deborah A. Stewart
Associate Academic Dean
Community College of Vermont

PART 1

The Community College Setting

History

In more than 100 years of existence, the American community college has changed the education landscape for millions. Joliet Junior College (JJC) began in Illinois in 1901 as an extension of the local high school. It served six students that year. Today, JJC enrolls more than 31,000 students in credit and noncredit courses. Nationwide, at least 100 million people have attended community colleges since 1901, according to the American Association of Community Colleges (AACC).

Throughout their history, community colleges have focused primarily on providing a range of students with access to high-quality, affordable education. The early community college was generally small and offered only a traditional liberal arts curriculum. Committed to meeting the needs of the community, these colleges in the 1930s responded to the Great Depression by offering employment programs and training. After World War II, community colleges enjoyed considerable growth. During the 1960s alone, more than 450 new community colleges opened their doors (American Association of Community Colleges [AACC], 2001). According to Coley (2000), "[t]his tremendous expansion was fueled by the push for universal education, the GI Bill, the baby boom, the civil rights movement, the nation's needs for worker training, and a robust national economy" (p. 6). Today, there are more than 1,100 community colleges nationwide.

Decades of steady growth shaped the colleges' ability to respond to community needs with flexibility and innovation, all the while deepening the core values that were present from the beginning. These values include access and diversity. In addition, community colleges have long invested in the preparation of students for both transfer to bachelor's-degree programs and entry into a skilled workforce. When students discovered themselves to be unprepared to succeed in the classroom, community colleges built developmental or remedial education programs. They also sought out partnerships with high schools and technical education centers. Through all of this, community colleges have embraced varied and relevant curricula.

Although much has changed for community colleges in the past century, much has also stayed the same. Today's student and faculty populations are more diverse and more representative of society at large than were those of earlier eras, although an emphasis on teaching and learning remains at the heart of most missions. With increased accountability, community colleges also have moved closer toward the concept of "the learning college" (O'Banion, 1997, p. 47). And although community colleges embrace emerging technologies, they tend to view innovation through the lens of their own institutions, seeking to integrate and adapt methods that allow for greater access and an easing of the barriers that confront so many potential learners. New populations of students— younger students, international students, those students who have already achieved a degree, and new American students—continue to enrich and challenge the community college climate, expanding opportunities for vitality and growth.

Mission, Vision, and Values

Many community colleges place great store in their mission statements, revisiting them from time to time to ensure that what they say about their institutions continues to tangibly inform their planning objectives, academic initiatives, and day-to-day operations. The mission statement is an important guide to helping community colleges stay responsive to their communities. The mission statement succinctly and articulately describes the college's purpose, lays out its core values, and identifies whom it serves. By contrast, the vision statement enables colleges to look forward—to what they want to become and how they might get there. A list of values or value statements provides even more detail as colleges identify the priorities or commitments that shape them as institutions. Understanding a college's philosophy and values is essential for instructors in determining the best setting for their work.

Mission

Each community college has its own mission statement, but there are many similarities. In general, community colleges address the ideals of open access, low cost, service to and partnership with the community, open admissions, and lifelong learning, including developmental education. A sampling of mission statements across the spectrum of community colleges and community college systems illustrates these ideals.

> "At Central Texas College, we identify and serve our unique, global community needs and provide quality teaching through an accessible learning environment."

> "Community College of Vermont is committed to serving and working with people to realize their learning, life, and career goals through access, excellent academic programs, and support. We are guided by respect for, and active engagement with, our diverse communities and the broad spectrum of learning needs in and beyond Vermont."

> "Joliet Junior College is committed to providing a quality education that is affordable and accessible to the diverse student population it serves. Through a rich variety of educational programs and support services, JJC prepares its students for success in higher education and employment. As part of this College's commitment to lifelong learning and services to its community, it also provides a broad spectrum of transitional, extension, adult, continuing and workforce education."

> "Kauai Community College [HI] is an open access, postsecondary institution that serves the community of Kauai and beyond. We provide education/training in a caring, student-focused, and intellectually stimulating environment. This education/training contributes to the development of lifelong learners who think critically, appreciate diversity, and lead successful, independent, socially responsible, and personally fulfilling lives."

> "The Maricopa Community Colleges [AZ] create and continuously improve affordable, accessible, effective, and safe learning environments for the lifelong educational needs of the diverse communities we serve."

> "Tompkins Cortland Community College [NY] makes it possible for people to identify and achieve their educational goals by providing accessible, quality, postsecondary education and training."

"West Valley College [CA] is a public community college whose primary purpose is to facilitate successful learning. It is committed to the education of the individual along with fostering the economic development of the communities it serves. West Valley College provides students with opportunities to participate in a wide spectrum of educational experiences designed to fulfill their academic and career needs. Encouraged to seek knowledge and wisdom as lifelong learners, our students are motivated to expand their human potential, enrich the quality of their lives, and develop the job skills and other competencies necessary to function in contemporary society."

All these colleges see themselves as learning communities. Hence their missions address both a learner's access to and success in the classroom. In addition, community colleges see the role of education as a lifelong endeavor; thus, these mission statements focus on providing opportunities for students to move in and out of higher education as academic and workplace needs develop and are addressed. In short, the mission of community colleges is to serve both individual learners and their communities. As Bailey and Averianova (1999) have asserted, "No other institution has demonstrated so much flexibility in adapting to the community's needs" (p. 5).

> *In short, the mission of community colleges is to serve both individual learners and their communities.*

Vision

Vision statements articulate where institutions want to be and how they will get there. As a result, there is a good deal of variety in the vision statements of community colleges. Some colleges aspire to a concrete and singular goal such as being the best college in a particular region or area. Other colleges use language that is more internally focused. For instance, the vision of the University of Kentucky-Lexington Community College is "to become one of the top 20 community colleges in the United States." Orange Community College's (NY) vision statement includes the following:

"We will be the best college in the SUNY System, the college of choice for all Orange County citizens....We welcome all as individuals, ensure academic and intellectual challenge, and mentor all in a caring, supportive environment. Students will remember the College as one of their most richly rewarding experiences, the compass that guides their continued development. We consistently renew our promise to be a most rigorous and caring academic institution, to provide visionary leadership, and to create a symphony of opportunity for personal and professional growth. We aspire to be the most efficient in shepherding public resources and to be a strategic force in enhancing the quality of life in Orange County and beyond."

Wallace Community College-Selma (GA) articulates its vision as follows:

"The College shares a vision of student-centered educational excellence that is responsive to the needs of our service area and is manifested by quality teaching, educational support services, and access to opportunity. Challenged by change and innovation, we will move forward to create a future responsive to the diverse needs of students, community and state."

The Community College of Vermont (CCV) and Maricopa Community Colleges, among others, have vision statements that focus on their responsiveness, respectfulness, and use of resources in accomplishing their goals as learning institutions. Although community colleges may express their goals differently, the truth is that they share many of the same values.

Values

In carrying out their missions and fulfilling their visions, community colleges often are guided by a set of shared values that assist them in staying committed to students, constituents, and their own sense of purpose. Although each college expresses these values in its own way, they often fall into six major categories: learning, teaching, excellence, diversity, leadership, and technology.

LEARNING This is the first value espoused by many colleges, and it may, in fact, be broken down into multiple values that encompass both access and quality. Some colleges identify the lifelong learner by name here, and they also articulate the kinds of learning they want to promote, namely experiential or active learning. For instance, Arapahoe Community College (CO) declares that it values "upholding the highest academic standards and supporting the personal growth of each individual—ideals that nurture lifelong learning and an entrepreneurial spirit." University of Hawai'i-Kauai Community College describes two of the values through which it meets its mission: "[t]imely and timeless learning, both practical and theoretical, comprehensive and accessible to students of all ages and backgrounds" and "[a]n appreciation for intellectual pursuits which fosters in...students the ability to analyze problems, think critically, and communicate ideas effectively through writing, speech, and/or an artistic medium."

TEACHING Because a high priority is placed on teaching at community colleges, it is not surprising to find this value commonly articulated in a college's strategic statements. Sometimes it is expressed concisely, the way Tompkins Cortland Community College does, as "excellence in teaching." Jackson Community College (MI) values the kind of teaching that "produce[s] the greatest learning." Other colleges include teaching and learning activities that happen outside the traditional classroom. The Community College of Vermont states: "We recognize education as a positive social change agent in the attainment of equity; we commit to striving for excellence in our classrooms and all learning settings." In addition, some colleges include support staff and other personnel for their contributions to the learning environment.

EXCELLENCE Excellence is often mentioned in conjunction with teaching and learning, but it also is identified as a general value for institutions, covering aspects as diverse as community responsiveness, assessment, innovation, risk-taking, and academic standards. The Coastal Georgia Community College describes "a commitment to excellence and responsiveness within a scope of influence defined by the needs of a local area and by particularly outstanding programs or distinctive characteristics that have a magnet effect throughout the region or state." Maricopa Community Colleges frame their value as an invitation to the entire community: "We invite innovation, support creative problem-solving, and encourage risk-taking. We value teamwork, cooperation, and collaboration as a part of our continuous improvement efforts."

DIVERSITY Community colleges tend to be more racially and ethnically diverse than are four-year colleges (Coley, 2000). However, diversity is not just a by-product of open access, which manifests itself in low tuition and open admissions. Many community colleges embrace what diversity offers them as learning communities, and for years community colleges have sought out new audiences for teaching and learning. It is no surprise then that so many colleges articulate values of diversity and inclusiveness. Arapahoe Community College describes its focus on integrity as "the free exchange of ideas in an environment that embraces honesty, personal responsibility, as well as intellectual and cultural diversity."

A number of community colleges view diversity as Coastal Georgia Community College does, as embodying "the ideals of an open, democratic, and global society." Tidewater Community College (VA) emphasizes cultural diversity as important for students in meeting "the changing needs of a pluralistic, democratic society." Mesa Community College (AZ) defines inclusiveness in terms of both individuals and their ideas, and goes on to state: "We respect the dignity of each individual, expressed through fairness and just treatment for all. We value individual diversity and recognize the unique contributions of all individuals. We promote open communication and the free exchange of thoughts and ideas."

LEADERSHIP Community colleges take seriously the responsibility of fostering the development of students, faculty, and staff. Transformative learning—that is, engaging in learning that challenges one's values and belief systems—is important to personal development (Mezirow, 1991, 1997). For example, CCV "strive[s] for a learning and working environment that fosters the growth of each individual," encouraging the ability to "set goals and take risks." For community colleges, active leadership is promoted at all levels of the institution and is connected to partnerships with the community at large. A defining feature of community colleges is their responsiveness. Tidewater Community College describes its efforts to create "[p]artnerships and proactive responsiveness to develop cutting-edge programs that meet the changing needs of students and industry, while contributing to the economic, civic, and cultural vitality of the region, the Commonwealth, the nation, and the international community." Maricopa Community Colleges address leadership values of being self-reliant and accountable when they state: "We believe employees are accountable for their personal and professional actions as they carry out their assignments. We are all responsible for making our learning experiences significant and meaningful. We are accountable to our communities for the efficient and effective use of resources."

TECHNOLOGY Issues surrounding technology—namely, how much and what kinds—create challenges for community colleges just as they do for all organizations. However, a long-standing history of access, flexibility, and change make the community college receptive to technology's role in education, especially as it reduces barriers, addresses students' learning needs, and enhances the administrative aspects of serving students and faculty. Colleges such as University of Hawai'i-Maui Community College, charged with providing higher education to students in remote areas, turned the challenge of reaching students into an expertise in teleconferencing. Other community colleges have done likewise.

According to Parrott (1995), as early as 1994, "80% of community colleges in the United States offered some form of distance education" (para.1). Thus, a number of colleges address the use of technology as an educational and institutional tool in their values. University of Hawai'i-Kauai Community College promises to meet its mission through, among other things, the "[c]reative synergies of curriculum and programs that maximize the use of technology for global reach and adaptability to change." In building its vision, Jackson Community College "[e]mploys technology extensively in the learning process and supports that technology." Edison Community College (FL) provides "[a]ccessibility to programs through academic advising, flexible scheduling, and distance education." Whether colleges focus on technology's role in enhancing learning or enhancing access to learning, most see the value of being innovative as integrally linked to technology..

The Role of Student Development

For those who work and teach at community colleges, an important goal is to help students become self-reliant adults who know how to learn individually and through cooperation with others. When students leave our colleges, we want them to be effective learners and citizens who have built a strong foundation of academic, critical-thinking, and collaborative skills that they can use to learn a new subject, adapt to changing circumstances, and fulfill their career and personal aspirations. Therefore, the education we offer is integrally connected to the transformation of students as learners.

To enhance the development of students, our colleges provide a rich array of services and programs, everything from academic and financial counseling to support labs, freshman seminars, and mentoring opportunities. From a teaching perspective, instructors can provide learning experiences that are balanced between the needs of the learner and the requirements of the college, between subject matter content and academic skills, and between the theoretical and the practical. Ideally, students should get the sense of a discipline so they know its modes of inquiry and the sense of a subject so they understand what they do and do not know.

Inquiry does not begin free of values, assumptions, or perspectives (Hesse, 1980); thus, teaching for student development is multidimensional. Instructors should plan and teach their subjects in ways that provide opportunities for students to develop skills and awareness that transcend individual course goals. For instance, instructors can present students with real-life problems for building skills and reflecting on them. They can create collaborative classroom activities where students achieve early success and feel empowered to take risks. They can provide a syllabus or outline for their courses, including a list of learning objectives or goals. In addition, there are a number of "unwritten" objectives associated with any course: students should gain an understanding of themselves as learners, develop familiarity with a subject, and reinforce their critical-thinking skills. Instructors also can act as powerful role models for students, sharing their passion for learning and love of subject.

> *Can students, while learning the subject, also develop their critical-thinking skills, reason abstractly, solve problems, and communicate effectively? Will our courses encourage each student to develop an inquiring mind and a disposition toward lifelong learning?*

It seems certain that we will continue to see profound changes in the ways we earn a living. Postmodern organizations, including community colleges, find themselves constantly changing and adapting (Martin, 1999). This makes it all the more imperative that we prepare students for the rapidly changing circumstances that await them. We cannot know what will be required of them as the 21st century unfolds, but we do know that learning how to learn will be a necessity. In fact, a philosophy of developing students who can take charge of their own learning is in keeping with the shifting paradigm in higher education that calls for an emphasis on learning as linked to development. The question before many of us is, How can we as instructors do our part to provide the kind of education that is right for today's students?

Whatever courses we teach, it is important to divide our attention between the subject matter involved and what is happening to students as they engage with the content. We must consider ways that our courses can play a part in the development of the student. Can students, while learning the subject, also develop their critical-thinking skills, reason abstractly, solve problems, and communicate effectively? Will our courses encourage each student to develop an inquiring mind and a disposition toward lifelong learning? Will our courses provide skills students can use as they seek careers and employment?

Teaching for student development means teaching students the kinds of skills that will take them beyond our classrooms. Attending to a student's cognitive development is expanding her or his capacity to handle a broader range of subject matter while learning the content of the course. Teaching for development also provides students the opportunities to set goals, demonstrate active engagement, identify and address individual learning needs, build decision-making skills, and participate in an inclusive community. These opportunities not only encourage a student's educational growth, they honor the other contexts of a learner's life, including those of family, work, and community. All our students can benefit if we develop a rich intellectual and emotionally supportive classroom environment that asks students to actively participate in the learning process and provides frequent feedback on their learning.

Principles for Good Teaching

Chickering and Gamson's (1987) "Seven Principles for Good Practice in Undergraduate Education" have been almost universally embraced by both colleges and faculty and have been adapted for use in legal education, student affairs, distance learning programs, teaching workshops, and other contexts. A number of community colleges include the principles as part of their Web site materials on teaching and learning, among them University of Hawai'i-Honolulu Community College, Community College of Rhode Island, Grand Rapids Community College (MI), and Glendale Community College (AZ). According to Chickering and Gamson (1987), good practice in undergraduate education "encourages contact between students and faculty, develops reciprocity and cooperation among students, encourages active learning, gives prompt feedback, emphasizes time on task, communicates high expectations, and respects diverse talents and ways of learning" (p. 1).

The Community College of Vermont (CCV) uses these seven principles as inspiration in articulating its own guidelines. CCV's "Principles of Good Teaching and Learning" shares a similar commitment to honoring the ways that students learn. The best teaching and learning occurs when the following occur.

- The classroom climate is one of mutual respect among all participants. It is a primary responsibility of CCV instructors to foster and exhibit respect for all students in the classroom, and to hear every student's voice, especially those that have been silenced in previous educational settings. Respect involves a recognition of different points of view, values, styles of learning, talents, and kinds of intelligence.

- Students are motivated. The stronger the desire to learn something, the more learning will occur. Instructors who display genuine passion for their subject matter and communicate high standards can generate a similar enthusiasm among students. Love of learning is the strongest motivation we can provide to our students.

- The learning environment in the classroom is treated as a holistic, dynamic system designed to accommodate different ways of learning and knowing. Instructional methods should promote a cycle of learning that includes opportunities for direct, hands-on experience; for reflection through reading, writing, and discussion; for students to derive personal meaning or make connections to their daily lives; and for discovering direct applications for the learning. The deepest learning states often occur when the whole brain is engaged, when analytical left-brain processes are accompanied by a range of right-brain understandings.

- Content is presented with the big picture first as a context for the specific, differentiated information of the subject. The most meaningful learning generally occurs when students have a context for specific content they are trying to learn. This content—information, material, or activities—should be connected either to broader student foundational concepts or to students' personal experiences. Learning that lacks a contextual framework tends to be superficial and of short duration.

- The class encourages dialogue and collaboration among students as well as between students and the instructor. Dialogue among classroom participants allows for the integration of new knowledge with what students already know, which in turn generates further understandings and fresh insights. Interactions among students and teachers can be the most effective triggers of meaningful learning.

- The class provides opportunities for direct experience and active application of course content. Students generally learn things best if they experience them first-hand or apply them directly to solve a problem. Providing students with opportunities to teach others what they are learning is one of the most effective ways to accomplish this kind of applied learning in the classroom.

- Student development and transformation becomes an intentional goal of the teaching and learning process. Student development involves positive changes in students' frames of reference and their ability to think critically and abstractly. This transformation is most likely to occur in an environment that includes safety and trust and provides occasional experiences of cognitive dissonance (i.e., experiences that lead students to question their own taken-for-granted beliefs and frames of reference).

- Assessment is an ongoing process that provides prompt feedback to students about their learning. Assessment is most effective when there is the least anxiety and the maximum potential to learn from the assessment procedure. Hence, students should perceive assessment as a natural and ongoing part of the cycle of learning.

The Community College Curriculum

From the beginning, the community college curriculum has focused on liberal arts and preparing students for transfer, although, according to Cohen and Brawer (2003), many leaders also advocated at the outset for increased emphasis on vocational or occupational education. Shifts in focus took place in the 1970s, when the curriculum narrowed to encompass more introductory courses and specialized noncredit classes, and again in the 1990s, when there was an expansion in offerings related to ethnic and cultural studies, religion, and music (Cohen & Brawer, 2003). Vocational/occupational programs—including those in early childhood education, laser optics, telecommunications, multimedia technology, dental hygiene, and radiology—are thriving in today's community colleges as institutions "keep pace with the changing skills needed in the workplace" (Coley, 2000, p. 18).

Instructors themselves can have an impact on enriching the curriculum, especially in those cases where they design and market courses of a particular interest. As Cohen and Brawer noted, "Faculty members who have determined to break away from their lecture and textbook course offerings have been able to do imaginative college-level work with their students" (2003, p. 323).

The Center for the Study of Community Colleges (CSCC) regularly surveys community colleges, conducting reviews of their catalogs and course schedules in order to track changes in the curriculum. Striplin (2000, p. 2) drew on the results of the 1998 CSCC study, *A Review of Community College Curriculum Trends*, in order to present the following highlights:

- Although enrollment in 1998 was comparable to that of 1991, nearly 30,000 more course sections were offered in 1998.

- The majority (54%) of course sections in the curriculum were in the liberal arts. From a long-range view, English and social science courses were relatively stable in growth, whereas science offerings have fluctuated over the years. Between 1991 and 1998, more colleges offered fine and performing arts courses.

■ At least 90% of the community colleges taking part in the survey offered courses in business, office management, marketing, health sciences, computer applications, and education. Students enrolled in computer science courses increased, overall, from 2% in 1991 to 4% in 1998.

The Associate Degree

More than 575,000 associate degrees were awarded in 2000–01, an increase of 20% since 1990, according to the National Center for Educational Statistics (NCES, 2003). In addition, the most popular associate degree awarded was in the area of liberal arts and sciences, general studies, and the humanities. More than one third (34%) of the total associate degrees awarded were in this field. The list of top fields includes, in order,

■ Liberal arts and sciences, general studies, and humanities

■ Business management and administration services

■ Health professions and related sciences

■ Engineering-related technologies

■ Computer and information sciences

■ Visual and performing arts

■ Protective services

■ Mechanics and repairers

■ Precision production trades

■ Multi/interdisciplinary studies

■ Education

One of the most important aspects of lists such as this is their fluidity and range. For example, the field of computer and information sciences accounted for 7,700 and 9,700 associate degrees in 1990–91 and 1995–96, respectively, but by 2000–01 this number had nearly tripled to 26,300 (NCES, 2003).

General Education Program

Colleges and universities expect students to complete general education courses in addition to the specific courses required for their degrees. This is important in helping students to develop, among other skills, greater breadth in their learning. In addition, general education requirements also reflect a college's values, what it believes is important for students to know or be able to do after graduation. Often these general education requirements include coursework in math, science, communication, humanities, and social sciences. Sometimes they also include courses in diversity, multiculturalism, or global perspectives.

Hudson Valley Community College (NY) outlines ten knowledge and skill areas for students including those in math, natural sciences, social sciences, American history, western civilization, other world civilization, the arts, humanities, foreign language, and communication. Montcalm Community College (MI) articulates eight general education competencies and identifies the courses that will satisfy them; graduates are expected to demonstrate

- proficiency in written and oral communication;

- awareness and understanding of the physical world and the scientific method;

- awareness and understanding of culture and society in general;

- awareness and understanding of global interdependence and the interrelation of communities, states, nations, economies, and peoples;

- awareness and understanding of and proficiency in computational methods and mathematical concepts and applications;

- understanding of and proficiency in the application of the tools of information technology to personal and professional work;

- proficiency in critical and creative thinking, learning to learn, and problem-solving; and

- ethical consideration in political, social, professional and personal endeavors.

Although it is useful for instructors to know where their courses fit institutionally and how they dovetail with other courses in the curriculum, it is especially important to understand the role of general education across curricular disciplines. General education competencies or outcomes may be best addressed when integrated throughout various courses. Cohen (1993) cited Eaton's assertion that an integration of general education with liberal arts or occupational course materials can assist students in developing "habits of thought" that "strengthen their reasoning capacity, their awareness of social and civic relationships and responsibilities, and their attention to values and moral issues" (para. 4).

Developmental Skills Program

Because access is a core value, the majority of community colleges have open admissions. This means, of course, that students who enter may be underprepared for college-level work. According to a survey conducted by AACC, 36% of students new to higher education at all types of institutions in the fall of 1998 were enrolled in at least one remedial course (Shults, 2000). In addition, students enrolled in two-year public colleges may spend more time on average in remedial courses than may students at public four-year colleges (Harris, 2004). The reasons behind this are complex. Coley (2000) suggested that remedial needs may be a result of factors in the student's familial or educational background, a learning disability, a language barrier, time away from a formal educational setting, or a change in employment. Whatever the reasons, community colleges have responded with the formation and expansion of developmental skills programs, recognizing that proficiency in reading, writing, and math is critical to a student's academic success.

Students are placed in developmental skills courses through various means, depending on the college. Many institutions give placement exams, although some colleges administer these exams only to entering freshmen who show signs of problems, such as low SAT scores or grade point averages. In general, students need more development in math than in reading and writing. This is especially true in two-year colleges where 35% of freshmen in fall 2000 were enrolled in remedial math courses, compared with 8% to 18% of freshmen who enrolled in such courses at other types of institutions (Harris, 2004). Basic skills courses are often taught by faculty in the academic departments related to the discipline, and, frequently, colleges rely on technology in their efforts to serve students in this area. Two-year public colleges are in fact more likely than are four-year colleges to offer basic-skills courses through distance education and to "use computers as a hands-on instructional tool" (Harris, 2004, para. 12).

However, what may be most important from an instructor's perspective is the way all teaching and learning can be enriched through consideration of the areas of overlap between developmental and other education. Franke (cited in Cohen, 1993) argued that general education instructors can benefit from learning "the cross-curricular techniques of developmental education, including writing across the curriculum, content area reading, or applied mathematics," whereas basic skills instructors can learn "from general education practitioners the means of introducing higher-order thinking skills into developmental students' first courses" (para. 8). In addition, Rose (1989) argued eloquently against seeing students' writing in the pathological terms suggested by "remedial." Instead, Rose suggested that we provide students—all students, but especially those who are underprepared—with the opportunity to think about and practice the language of academic discourse, which includes talking and writing about their learning, developing strategies that are related to academic inquiry, and discussing the areas where ideas and beliefs may clash. In short, we need to recognize the role of culture in our classrooms. And although it is a mistake to imagine that students enrolled in a developmental writing course are incapable of thinking critically about a history topic, it is also a mistake to imagine that students in a history course would not benefit from activities that reinforce the skills of writing and reading. Students in both types of courses would benefit from reflecting on themselves as learners.

A similar case can be made for the overlap of developmental and general education with occupational or technical education. Students who enter the workforce need to think critically, communicate well, and reason quantitatively. They also need to develop individual strategies for learning new information and skills. When we as instructors are finally able to see the benefits of sharing methods across the curriculum, perhaps we will see students better able to integrate and transform their learning from course to course.

Industry Skills and Standards

Along with academic skill standards, community colleges today are increasingly influenced by industry-skill standards, standards that come from the world of work, not from the world of classrooms. Degree programs, where relevant, often are aligned with professional and industry standards. In the end, however, the division between academic skill standards and industry skill standards may be largely artificial; whenever employers are asked what skills they want in new workers, they almost always include general academic skills along with any industry-specific standards. Employers want to hire people who can speak and write clearly, who can think quantitatively, who can work in teams, who can solve problems, and who can research and analyze information.

Of interest to many instructors is whether students learn any better when they are held accountable to clearly articulated standards of various kinds. More and more classroom research indicates that they do, that students achieve better results and learn more when standards are explicit and set at the right level. Set standards too low and they lose their value. Set them too high and they become a meaningless rhetorical exercise.

Moreover, no matter how perfectly they are written, in the end we know that standards by themselves are not enough. Teachers still must teach. Students still must study and strive. The standards are only standards—like a skeleton—not much use without the breath and spirit of living beings, students and teachers, engaged in discovery, problem solving, and thinking.

Community College Students

General Characteristics

In thinking about issues of teaching and learning, it is essential to begin with the student. When we recognize students' diverse starting points, the rich life experiences they bring, and the different ways in which they learn and grow, we can better develop classroom environments that engage and nurture them. Students are certainly full partners in this process, but administrators and instructors provide the supports necessary to help all students succeed, regardless of their education goals.

Community college enrollment nationwide presents a portrait of rich and varied hues. According to the American Association of Community Colleges (AACC; Phillippe & Patton, 2000), most students attend college part time, and one-third of all students receive some type of financial aid. Enrollment is also greater among women than among men. Furthermore,

- More than 80% of students juggle both school and work. Nearly one-third of students attending classes full time also work full time, and among students aged 30–39, the percentage who work and attend college full time is 41% (p. 49).

- Minority students make up 30% of community college enrollments nationally. Students identifying themselves as Mexican, Mexican American, or Chicano make up the fastest growing racial/ethnic group (p. 38).

- The average age is 29; however, 32% of students are 30 or older, whereas 36% are 18–22, with a slight percentage (4%) younger than 18 (p. 30).

In addition, the approximately 6% of all undergraduates who reported having a disability, according to the 1995–96 National Postsecondary Student Aid Study (NPSAS), were more likely to attend a public two-year institution or other institution (such as a for-profit vocational institution) than a four-year public college or university (Hurst & Smerdon, 2000). Students reported having learning, orthopedic, hearing, vision, speech, or other health-related disabilities or impairments.

Current trends portend increasing diversity among community college students, with more high school students, reverse transfer students, and displaced workers enrolling (Andrews, 2003). A growing number of high school students are attending community colleges through dual-enrollment programs aimed at giving them a jump-start on college. In fact, the states of Washington, Arizona, and Iowa, to name just a few, have formal legislation regarding dual enrollment. Community colleges are also enrolling more students who arrive from four-year institutions. This phenomenon, called reverse transfer, includes both students who have earned a degree and may be looking for new skills and those who left a four-year institution without attaining a degree. Finally, although community colleges have long sought to serve students interested in job training, they also find themselves called upon to serve students with retraining needs also. This population includes laid-off or underemployed workers, employees seeking to change careers, and employees whose companies are interested in developing their employees' technology skills. This population also includes welfare recipients who, as a part of state welfare-to-work programs, take part in job training and retraining, some of which is short-term (Andrews, 2003).

Diverse Students

Most community college classes contain a kaleidoscopic mix of students characterized by different ages, backgrounds, learning styles, educational experiences, and motivations. Because of this diversity, instructors cannot be certain that new students have attained the same minimum level of experience and knowledge of content. Instructors can, however, use this uncertainty as an opportunity to assess what students think and know early in the semester and to create the kinds of connections that benefit all students and the kind of learning community that builds on the collective experiences and knowledge of the whole class.

Students may also differ in ability and in previous academic achievement. It can be challenging to teach at a number of different levels within the same class. Some of the strategies that can be helpful in these circumstances are as follows:

PEER TEACHING Peer teaching in pairs or small groups can be effective in accommodating individual differences. As students at different levels and with different learning styles interact, they all seem to benefit. More-advanced students enhance their learning through the process of teaching and explaining their ideas. Students who are struggling with the material may be able to glean new strategies for learning through their interactions with peers. Additionally, peer teaching allows all students the greatest opportunity for retention—up to 90%, according to the Learning Pyramid (National Training Laboratories, n.d.).

SMALL GROUP ACTIVITIES As in peer teaching, splitting a whole class into small groups and furnishing them with a manageable task or mission can engender a successful learning experience for all. Small group activities allow students to practice their skills in the safety of the group, encouraging them to take risks and work collaboratively. The small group setting, when developed and used appropriately, can also provide students with the opportunity to practice empathy and share their differences.

CHOICE OF ASSIGNMENTS Because students approach subject knowledge and skills in different ways, it is important to offer them choice or variety in their assignments. For example, an English instructor might give students a choice of writing a short persuasive essay or a cover letter for a job application. A business instructor might ask students to do a market analysis of a product and write a paper, create a Web page, or give an oral presentation on the findings. Even if an instructor requires students to write an essay as a part of an exam, he or she can still give students a choice of three or four questions to respond to. The important point here is recognizing that students may approach learning in different but equally valid ways. In addition, we want to encourage students to be engaged in what they are learning, and this happens best when students have some choice in the process.

CHOICE OF LEARNING ACTIVITIES Just as it is important to offer students choice of assignments, it is also worthwhile to vary classroom activities to accommodate diverse learning styles. Instructors can employ visual, auditory, and hands-on methods for teaching content. They can also include experiential and small group discussion activities to supplement lecture and writing activities. Again, the importance here is in providing all students with the opportunity to be successful in the classroom. At the same time, by varying the activities in a class, we continue to challenge and engage all students. As Rodgers (1969) asserted, "The only learning which significantly influences behavior is self-discovered, self-appropriated learning. Such self-discovered learning, truth that has been appropriated and assimilated in experience, cannot be directly communicated to another" (p. 153).

Although students differ in many ways, there is no one single model for success in any academic or career field. In delivering this message, we have a responsibility to reflect on our own differences and the self or selves we carry with us into every classroom. We can describe our own challenges in the field. We also can introduce students to as many different role models as possible, whether they are in the form of guest speakers, readings, films, or case studies. In fact, we can create problem-solving opportunities for students in which they imaginatively take on the professional roles they desire. Last, we can encourage students to articulate their goals and dreams for the future and share them. In the end, diversity makes teaching at a community college both exciting and challenging.

New Students

Given that half of first-time college students attend a community college, it is likely that we all will encounter a new college student sometime in our teaching. This means we cannot assume students know any of our expectations. Furthermore, research indicates that the first six weeks of the semester are a critical period for new students; as a result, they may need some special attention during that period because they are still testing the waters to see if they can succeed in a college program. As we have learned over and over, nothing leads to continued success more often than early success. When we asked instructors at CCV to discuss what they do during the first six weeks of the semester to ensure that all students (new and veteran) have an academically engaging and successful experience in their classes, they came up with many terrific suggestions.

Build a Framework for the Course

It is important to give students the sense that the course has a solid structure or foundation.

As we have learned over and over, nothing leads to continued success more often than early success.

- Help students understand what they are going to learn and how they are going to learn it as a way of previewing the coming attractions in a course. Also, talk about learning how to learn, and give concrete examples of ways to learn.

- Prepare and provide a good syllabus, and stick to it—or announce any changes.

- Find out what students know about the subject, content, or skills before they begin learning in the course. This can be done in the first session or two through an in-class assessment, survey, personal writing, or group activity or game.

- When presenting information, begin with the concrete, and make sure everyone understands it before moving toward the abstract. Sequence assignments and quizzes purposefully to take advantage of how students learn.

- Deliver all course expectations in writing. Delineate all assignments.

- Introduce study skills into the syllabus. Before assigning the first paper, spend time in class talking about choosing a topic or building support. It could also be helpful to show examples and ask students to talk about their past experiences with writing papers. What have they learned to do (or not do) as a result of their experiences?

- Build assignments logically and carefully, providing opportunities for students to do meaningful work.

Give and Get Feedback

Assessment should be a natural and ongoing part of the learning cycle.

- Have students complete a one-minute assessment at the end of each class. This can be an opportunity to express confusion or frustration. It can also be an opportunity for them to share what really worked for them, what they think is most important, and even what thoughts they have about learning.

- Give a short quiz in each class, graded or not. Some instructors schedule extra quizzes for which students scoring 85% or better receive extra credit for their efforts. Extra-credit quizzes enable students to build their test-taking skills and their knowledge of the material in a win–win situation.

- Provide feedback on students' work in a timely manner, and be specific. It is important to provide extensive, or at least descriptive, comments on early assignments. This is especially important in the online classroom, where students look for written feedback on their contributions to the discussion. Always return work promptly.

- Compliment students publicly for good presentations or exam results, and be specific with the compliment. In fact, it is a good idea to find something positive and specific to say to each student in the class.

- Do quick in-class assessments of necessary skills; refer those who need help to the college's learning or writing center. In the online classroom, look to the discussion forum as a method for iterative and ongoing assessment of students' writing and thinking skills.

- Have an open-door policy; encourage students to share what they are thinking and how they are grappling with the course's goals. Before class begins, take a moment to ask how students are or how they felt about the homework.

- Balance the need for structure and consistency with flexibility in terms of the syllabus or agenda. If students are struggling over a concept or skill, take the time to address their confusion before moving on to the next step. Find the teachable moment in a class.

- Give students several chances to succeed with content. If students are not initially successful, give them an opportunity to convert a low grade to something closer to their personal goals.

- Encourage students to realize that there may be more than one solution to a problem or situation—or more than one way to get to a correct solution. Find ways to give credit for thinking rather than simply getting the right answer.

- Give out a list of hints with each homework assignment.

Establish Accountability

Students need to know that they are full partners and must take responsibility for their learning.

- Set clear standards for classroom behavior and stick to them.

- Assume it is the students' choice—and their priority—to be in class.

- Notify students about what to do when they miss a class. Establish expectations for them to pick up and drop off homework and make up missed work.

- Make it clear that we learn from each other and because of that, we need to attend each and every session.

- Be mindful that students may need to be taught good study habits, ethics, and standards.

Engage Students

Students learn more and retain more of their learning when they enjoy the process.

- Start each class with news items to show the connections between course work and the world around us. Use humor and metaphor to make unusual connections. These will help students to remember the material long after the course is over.

- Offer extra-help sessions.

- Use real-life problems or case scenarios to illustrate the kinds of learning that happen in the field and to get students excited about the work.

- Give students one-on-one attention so they can share issues, concerns, and fears. In addition, demonstrate your conviction that students can be successful in the course.

- Have students write down their expectations and their worst fears in the first class; hold onto these (in a sealed envelope) and return them to the students in the last class so they can mark their progress.

- Vary in-class activities: lecture, small group activities, independent writing exercises, videos, and games. Variety will keep students engaged in the learning and address all the different ways students can be successful in the class.

- Provide a (confidential) forum for sharing problems and issues related to the course, such as writing in student logs or journals and sharing obstacles in the learning. Address these disclosures with empathy and strategies for success.

Build a Learning Community

For some students, the simple sense of belonging gives them a powerful incentive to continue in their education.

- Model the process of taking risks and learning from mistakes. Provide opportunities for this to happen without penalty of a bad grade. For instance, encourage students to speculate and make mistakes in the classroom setting.

- Learn students' names as quickly as possible, and use them.

- Foster interaction among students at the first class and continue with each class. Solicit students' responses and opinions in each class.

- Find out in the beginning which students are new to college, and make a point of welcoming them. Use small group activities to pair new students with veteran students.

- Be active, engaging, and passionate. In the first class, share your background or interest in the subject. Introduce fun activities that will build the same passion and engagement in students.

- Use icebreakers for students, at least in the first class. Create a way for all students to contribute.

- Socialize during breaks. Demonstrate approachability with students.

- Encourage students to help other students.

- Create and nurture a nonjudgmental environment.

- Set ground rules that enable students to learn in a comfortable atmosphere. Articulate differences between criticism and critique.

High School Students

The number of dual-enrolled and dual-credit students increased in the 1990s. In general, dual-enrolled students are high school or secondary students enrolled in college courses for college credit, whereas dual-credit students are secondary students enrolled in courses that grant them both high school and college credit (Andrews, 2001). The reasons for such a movement are many, including the desire to enrich students' last two years of high school and create a bridge from secondary school to college for students at risk. The movement has proven to be popular; as Andrews (2003) reported, dual enrollments approach 500,000 in community colleges, with high program growth noted in numerous states. In 2003 the Bill and Melinda Gates Foundation made a $9 million commitment to the California Community Colleges to create 15 early-college high schools throughout the state.

In response, many community colleges have developed programs to guide and monitor progress, document learning, and support the rise of this new population. Colleges are keenly aware that many of these students require more dedicated academic, social, and life skills support. In addition, younger students often benefit from additional resources to foster their confidence, their capacity to succeed, and their aspirations.

In the classroom, much of what works for community college students works also for high school students. As part of a statewide mandate to identify the critical issues facing secondary schools in Vermont, the Vermont High School Task Force (2002), created a document called "High Schools on the Move," describing how all students can be fully engaged in their learning. As set out by the task force, all students need opportunities to do the following:

■ Communicate their understanding in a variety of ways

■ Make connections between theoretical knowledge or concepts and real-life applications

■ Act as self-reliant learners, assuming responsibility for their own decisions and actions

■ Work collaboratively and cooperatively with others to solve problems

■ Develop essential skills for lifelong learning in critical thinking, writing, speaking, and information literacy

■ Practice these essential skills in a safe learning environment

■ Express their learning in personalized and relevant ways

■ Articulate their goals for the future and build strategies for meeting them

■ Understand how they learn best and work on ways to apply this knowledge to their studies

■ Be engaged in their learning and develop independence and flexibility in their thinking

■ Work with instructors who understand that students need multiple pathways to success and are committed to using a variety of teaching methods in the classroom.

Dual enrollments approach 500,000 in community colleges, with high program growth noted in numerous states. In 2003 the Bill and Melinda Gates Foundation made a $9 million commitment to the California Community Colleges to create 15 early-college high schools throughout the state.

Traditional-Age and Older Adult Students

Although there is much that unites students at community colleges, there are differences in how traditional-age and older adult students tend to respond to instruction in an academic environment. These are generalizations, of course, and there are exceptions to every generalization. That said, younger students are more likely to see higher education as something that can be acquired, consumed, and accumulated, rather than as something that they help to create. For these students, the knowledge they get may have value mostly in terms of its currency in the marketplace.

Put another way, younger adults may, on the surface, be less concerned with a course's relevancy to their personal growth and more concerned with learning for the test, getting the grade, or accumulating the credit. Although they may see a course's content as potentially useful in the future, the immediate functionality of knowledge may not seem as important. Younger learners may not see the direct connection between going to school and undergoing any kind of personal transformation in the way they think about themselves or the world. Given community colleges' general educational aims, this can create some tension because of the mismatch between instructors' expectations and students' goals.

Younger students' approaches to learning have some positive aspects. Steitz (1985) wrote that separating one's self from the content can be a real advantage when it is necessary to focus on detail or memorize facts without regard to utility or meaning in relation to real-life situations. Younger students often can work fast and deal with a large quantity of questions in a testing situation, and they may have a greater facility with technology and multi-tasking (Steitz, 1985). These qualities may make a good fit with the demands of today's workplace. Still, this approach to learning may also translate into a passive style in the classroom.

Older adult learners seem naturally inclined to connect new learning to their previous experiences or apply it to some specific goal. In fact, these students may see a course as a step toward finding a better job, upgrading the one they have, or starting a new career—all very pragmatic.

Older adult learners seem naturally inclined to connect new learning to their previous experiences or apply it to some specific goal. In fact, these students may see a course as a step toward finding a better job, upgrading the one they have, or starting a new career—all very pragmatic. Many returning adults want to use education—put it to work, not just receive it. Their approach as they enter college may be, at least in their own minds, essentially practical. At the same time, however, many of these students also have an underlying desire to take control of their lives and to make a transformation they intuitively know is positive. They may be facing a life crisis—divorce, death of a spouse, empty nest, or loss of employment—and thus treat education as an active, positive response to a major transition in their lives. As a result, older adult learners are likely to see the many connections between school, personal growth, and change.

Many adult students have also reached a period in their lives when, for the first time, they realize that the time left to get an education is limited. As a result, and in contrast with younger students, they may feel pressed to make up for lost time, learn what they need quickly, and get on with the rest of their lives. When the rush to master learning conflicts with underdeveloped skills, these students may become frustrated and discouraged.

Older adults may have difficulty seeing themselves as students, not because they are not committed to their education but because they may have full-time responsibilities in addition to their course work. It may be very difficult for these students to find time for studying with peers, socializing with classmates, or engaging in extracurricular activities at the college. As a result, some students drop their courses or disappear from class without a word; the more connected we can stay with these students, the better. In addition, knowing that most students are quite busy in their lives can help us to become better instructors. In constructing and leading our classes, we can think about how to reach all students and effectively engage them. Here are some specific ways:

- Set high expectations, and clarify them. Students generally need and want to have high expectations placed on them. That high expectations and high achievement go hand in hand is well-documented in the education literature.

- Support and encourage students while providing them with challenging learning experiences. Most students enter college with a mixture of hope and fear. A little failure may lead to discouragement, whereas small successes can strengthen a student's courage and resolve. Instructors can also help to convince students that failure to pass a course does not always indicate lack of aptitude. For some students, registering for one class is a major success—a small step toward a college education. It may take one or two tries to pass a course—successes may come in small but steady increments—and our encouragement for the things students do well may be the foundation on which eventual success can be built.

- Use a variety of teaching methods. Whereas younger students may prefer exploring a breadth of topics in a survey or introductory course, older students may want to explore certain topics in more detail. Instructors can accommodate both preferences by introducing case studies and real-life issues or problems into the class. Instructors can also encourage students to keep track of interesting topics for their own independent projects. Finally, encourage students to take responsibility for one or two topics in a semester, developing questions for discussion and connections to real-life that can be shared with the whole class.

- Use groups to celebrate diversity in the classroom. A proven method for developing students' appreciation for their differences is to combine students in small groups in which individual differences can be used to support the goal or task of the group.

- Create meaningful and relevant assignments that provide opportunity for reflection. Although younger students may have difficulty seeing the transformative qualities of their education, they do want to be engaged and find personal satisfaction or meaning in their learning. The more opportunities we provide for all students in this regard, the more ownership they feel over their learning.

- Provide opportunities for students to share and question their frames of reference. We can begin by reflecting on our own frames of reference. Failing to do this, we allude to certain events or ideas as though everyone knows about them, and we risk alienating students. This is not just true for students of different ages. To further encourage critical thinking, we can ask students, at certain moments, to step outside their own particular ethnocentric and egocentric limits—enough to see and appreciate another's point of view. And we can do the same.

Adult Development Theory

In the past 30 or 40 years, research on human cognition and neuroscience has changed educators' understanding of adult learning. Beginning in the 1960s, the literature on adult learning has expanded to include a wide array of cognitive and learning style models that illustrate how adults learn in different modes (e.g., Belenky, Clinchy, Goldberger, & Tarule, 1986; Briggs & Myers, 1977; Entwhistle, 1988; Klein, Riley, & Schlesinger, 1962; Kolb, 1984; McCarthy, 1996; Rayner & Riding; 1997; Witkin & Goodenough, 1981). Complementing new learning and cognitive style models is Gardner's (1983, 1993) work on multiple intelligences. New understandings gained from studies of adults as learners have helped to shift the emphasis in higher education from what is taught to what is learned and how students change through the process of learning.

We now know that adults go through phases in the life cycle just as children go through phases in growing up. However, the timetables for the adult phases may be less predictable, and various labels have been given to these stages. What we can say with some confidence is that many adults, at different points in their lives, experience periods of questioning and reevaluation.

Although these questioning periods can be difficult, they often translate into serious self-reflection and change. Many community college students are engaged in the process of reevaluating their situations and their lives and have decided that returning to school can potentially improve their lives. In addition, the sense of being in flux or in transition is carried into the classroom by many students and becomes a factor in the teaching–learning process. For example, some students may be afraid of succeeding, because success means leaving behind their old lives and ways of thinking. Other students may be eager to question and abandon truths they previously held. Their classroom discussions may be richer but may also be characterized by dissonance.

The good news is that as students address the issues and problems arising at different points in the life cycle, they also have the potential to change the ways in which they perceive themselves and the world. In other words, students can change their basic perspectives on reality, the ways in which they think about learning, and the ways in which they reason about things in general. With life experience and education, people can develop new frames of reference by which they perceive the world. Intellectual development was first noticed in children by the Swiss psychologist and biologist Jean Piaget. Piaget observed that as children developed, they would periodically undergo major changes in the way they reasoned about and acted on things and events in their environments.

Because intellectual development has such a significant impact on how students learn, it is important to realize that the stages represent the positions students take in how they perceive their own realities, including the subjects we teach. Perry (1999), a pioneer in the field, described nine positions or stages in a student's intellectual and ethical development, which can be encapsulated in four main categories: duality, multiplicity, relativism, and commitment. These positions are like personal paradigms—influencing dramatically how individuals learn and interact intellectually with the world. The way in which a student understands and reasons has a direct and powerful influence on the teaching and learning process.

Learning that has the potential to change not only what we think but how we see ourselves is often referred to as transformational learning, a concept important to adult learning.

According to Surrey (1991), studies on mostly male subjects emphasize elements of independence, ambition, assertiveness, and competitiveness as a way of achieving success. Belenky et al. (1986) asserted that women's perspectives or ways of knowing are distinct in certain aspects. Women perceive themselves and the world through five stages characterized by elements of voice, moving from the first stage of silence, or difficulty defining oneself, to the final stage of constructed knowledge, where one has developed a fully integrated self (Belenky et al., 1986).

In general, people learn to think and reason in increasingly complex ways over time and with the right kinds of experiences. We become less sure that life consists of rights and wrongs and blacks and whites. We begin to question authorities and develop a healthy skepticism about what we read. As our thinking matures, we begin to see that evidence is needed to support an argument and that specific procedures are used to gain particular kinds of knowledge. We may find that our old way of understanding no longer accounts for all the new events, information, and ideas we encounter. We either have to reject what we are experiencing, attempt to alter it to fit our existing ideas (Piaget called this *assimilation*), or alter our way of thinking to *accommodate* this new learning. Put simply, our beliefs about the way things are can get challenged enough so that we become confused and *disequilibrated*.

Learning that has the potential to change not only what we think but how we see ourselves is often referred to as transformational learning, a concept important to adult learning (Boyd, 1991; Brookfield, 1987; Cranton, 1994; Daloz, 1986; Mezirow, 1991, 1997). As Mezirow (1991) wrote, "Transformative learning involves reflectively transforming our beliefs, attitudes, opinions, and emotional reactions"—those elements that make up our meaning "schemes" or "perspectives" (p. 223). Brookfield (1987) cited phases of transformative learning that include a "trigger event," "appraisal" of oneself or the issue, "exploration" of different ways of thinking or behaving, "developing alternative perspectives," and "integration" (p. 27).

In college, we often are exposed to new information and ideas that do not fit our previously established personal assumptions about what is true. If, for example, we have assumed that what is printed in textbooks is true, and then find that different textbooks provide conflicting information about the same topic, we may start to question our previous assumption that if something is published, it must be true. Because college exposes people to differing opinions and a wealth of new ideas, college is a good setting for intellectual development.

In a typical community college class, students can be found at different stages of intellectual development and will exhibit different ways of thinking. In fact, each student views knowledge and truth from a unique and individual perspective. These differing perceptions will profoundly influence how students receive and act on what is taught by instructors or what is presented in textbooks. It is clear that, as instructors, we face challenges when confronted with a classroom of students who, as individuals, have very different ways of knowing and looking at things. How can we help students to see beyond simple answers and certainties? How can we encourage students to question their own views on truth and knowledge? After all, it can be difficult and upsetting to give up one's old, more comfortable, and perhaps simpler perspectives.

Like climbing a ladder, the higher we get, the less secure we may feel in our position. However, as we gain new perspectives and grow intellectually, the world becomes a larger, more interesting place. As a consequence, it offers much greater potential for enriching experiences. If it is part of human nature to learn, grow, and develop, then the educational experience must stimulate and facilitate that process. In fact, questioning our own views may be the most important thing we can do for our students and ourselves. As Moore (n.d.) wrote, the work of Perry and other theorists "underscores the notion that the most powerful learning, the learning most faculty really want to see students achieve as a result of their college experiences, involves significant qualitative changes in the learners themselves" (para. 6).

Applying Adult Development Theory to Teaching

Adult development theory has significant implications for community college instructors. The fact that many adult students are going through life transitions frequently translates into a strong motivation for learning. Simply by creating an environment where students actively engage with new ideas, we can stimulate their intellectual growth. If we can relate the course content to learners' experiences and goals, we can facilitate this period of growth and increase the amount of learning that occurs.

Adult development models also help us to see why some students attempt to use concrete reasoning patterns to learn concepts that require more abstract thinking. The models can help us to be more sensitive to the gaps between the way material is presented and the readiness of some students to receive it. An instructor who is aware of developmental distinctions will translate the material for those students into more concrete terms or sequence the subject matter so that it progresses from the more familiar and concrete to the less familiar and more abstract. Students who believe that academic knowledge is the property of textbook authors and instructors will resist discussion periods, especially in small groups where the instructor may not be present. They see their role as receivers of information, not as creators of new knowledge. The informed instructor can demonstrate to these students that thinking and reasoning skills can be gained through interaction among students and between students and instructor.

According to Taylor, Marienau, and Fiddler (2000), "a mark of development is the capacity to see oneself, particularly one's beliefs and ideas, from multiple perspectives" (p. 36). Although biases and ways of thinking can be largely invisible and can act as impediments, dialogue—especially a "dialogical relationship to the self"—can help one to see these limitations for what they are (Taylor et al., 2000, p. 36). There are many ways of encouraging and stimulating students' development, although Daloz (1986) suggested that effective mentors—a term that encompasses instructors and others "concerned with guiding development"—primarily do three things: "they support, they challenge, and they provide vision" (p. 212). To that end, we can use the following classroom strategies in support of student development:

■ Adopt a mixture of presentation styles and instructional methods—small groups for those who need connection, lectures for others, Socratic questioning for some, reaction papers for still others. Sheckley (1984) noted that traditional approaches to college teaching may be ineffective when used in class of diverse adult learners.

Adult development theory has significant implications for community college instructors. The fact that many adult students are going through life transitions frequently translates into a strong motivation for learning.

■ Challenge students and their worldviews to provoke new kinds of thinking. At the same time, support students' efforts with encouragement and intersperse easier material with more challenging material. Success breeds success. Finding the appropriate balance between challenge and support for each student is one of the most important aspects of teaching for student development.

■ Let students learn from each other with lots of opportunities for the exchange of ideas and for people to connect with each other over a topic or problem. We know that instructors cannot be all things to all students; however, instructors can be catalysts for learning in a classroom. One of the ways we can accomplish this is to give students plenty of opportunities to learn from each other.

■ Present real problems so that students can experience how knowledge is created from evidence that is produced in the classroom. This classroom-as-laboratory approach can supplement more traditional lecture methods to get students actively engaged. In a microcosmic sense, history students become historians and business students become managers right in the classroom.

■ Help students to understand the uncertainty and impermanence of what we read, see, and hear. We can also help students to see that each discipline has its own set of procedures and standards that it uses to determine the relative rightness or wrongness of information or answers to questions. Instead of asking students for the correct answer, ask them to present the evidence or reasoning behind the answers they select.

■ Create opportunities for students to develop insight and intuition around subjects. We cannot ascribe meaning for students; they need to do this for themselves. However, we can create a climate in which creative and intuitive thinking is encouraged. McCarthy (2000) asserted that as students develop a personal investment or value in learning, "they will merge the energy of their intuition with their reasoning power. Such synergy results in deep levels of comprehension" (p. 94). Young (1982) suggested that such comprehension can be accomplished through poetic writing, which triggers a different emotional and cognitive stance for the student, and "provides the freedom important to making imaginative connections and realizing values" (pp. 85–86).

PART 3

Course Planning
Throughout the Semester

Select a Textbook

In many colleges, instructors are required to select a textbook or supplementary reading for their courses. This important decision can profoundly affect teaching and learning, so begin the process early. Of course, one of the best resources for textbook selection is other faculty, most of whom will generously share their perceptions of and experiences with a particular book. Even when a textbook is already selected, it is a good idea to talk with other faculty and critically assess the book. You may find it necessary, for instance, to supplement the textbook with other viewpoints.

A textbook is a comfortable tool for instructors and a security blanket for some students, so going without one is worth considering only if you have a good selection of alternative resources available. According to Johnston (1988), director of Texas A&M's Center for Teaching Excellence, textbooks provide continuity and a relatively uniform body of basic information. He notes that a good textbook includes a lot of graphs, maps, and diagrams and presents a large amount of information efficiently. If used properly, a textbook can speed the integration of content, allowing more in-class time for applications, analysis, and problem solving.

Not all instructors choose to use textbooks. For one thing, textbooks have become increasingly more expensive, and the financial burden of buying books can be significant for students on tight budgets. For another, some instructors are concerned that textbooks often draw all of the conclusions for students and thus leave little room for creative thinking. Furthermore, textbooks can become outdated quickly or may offer a limited, biased perspective. For example, a textbook on computer programming may show very few illustrations of female programmers; one on early childhood development may show few male child-care providers. For community college instructors, textbooks written for 18-year-olds may also fall short of ideal, because they devote much of their content to providing a basic context that many adult students already have.

Because the marketplace provides many textbooks to choose from, a number of colleges have developed lists of recommended, if not required, textbooks in their most frequently offered courses. These lists are often developed by faculty committees that meet regularly. If instructors do choose a textbook, they must use it. Students complain bitterly, and rightly so, if they are asked to purchase an expensive textbook and the instructor rarely refers to it or uses it only in a denigrating manner. Of course, this does not mean that instructors should not present alternative viewpoints or perspectives. Nor should instructors necessarily feel compelled to cover all the information included in textbooks, given that this sometimes allows precious little time for original source materials and other enriching and supplemental resources.

In his classic book, *The Craft of Teaching: A Guide to Mastering the Professor's Art*, Eble (1977) recommended that instructors learn to use class time to clarify and supplement the textbook material rather than repeating what is in print; he asserted that reading assignments can act as better discussion starters in the next class and that instructors should ask students questions involving applications, analysis, synthesis, and problem-solving. In addition, Fulwiler (1982) outlined the value of having students use journals to capture their thinking about topics in their field. Writing in a journal can help students to summarize their own and others' ideas, focus their thinking, pose and solve problems, record responses to reading assignments, chart their progress in the course, and discuss their ideas with other students. Choosing the best textbook for your course is important, but thinking about how you will use that textbook in class may be more essential.

Develop a Syllabus

A syllabus may encompass institutional aspects of the course, including meeting information and relevant policies, but is usually more extensive and detailed. It often includes the instructor's contact information and office hours, a course description, a list of learning objectives, the assigned textbook(s), major course requirements, an outline of assignments and due dates, course philosophy and expectations, grading criteria, and the instructor's own policies on absence and late work. In many colleges, instructors are required to develop their syllabi and submit them well before the semester begins; in fact, they are often available online. Because the syllabus acts as a kind of contract between the instructor and the class, it needs to be developed thoughtfully and with purpose.

Because so many college students, regardless of age, have many responsibilities beyond the classroom, they need to know what will be asked of them in terms of assignments and exams in order to schedule their time and energies accordingly. Therefore, it is important to provide them with a clear map in the form of a syllabus. Creating a syllabus is also a good way for instructors to view the course as a whole, making sure that topics are manageable for each class session and that homework assignments have balance and variety. In addition, developing a syllabus allows instructors the opportunity to think about their teaching philosophy—everything from expectations for writing assignments to handling late assignments or absences can be addressed in the syllabus. Thinking about potential situations before we are confronted with them can alleviate problems down the road.

In his classic book, The Craft of Teaching: A Guide to Mastering the Professor's Art, Eble (1977) recommended that instructors learn to use class time to clarify and supplement the textbook material rather than repeating what is in print; he asserted that reading assignments can act as better discussion starters in the next class and that instructors should ask students questions involving applications, analysis, synthesis, and problem-solving.

Certain aspects of the syllabus may be standardized, although these vary from college to college. At some colleges, for example, the course description and learning objectives or outcomes are already determined for courses. At others, a blurb may be standardized for each course, but instructors can elaborate on this description and create their own outcomes. It may be helpful to view sample syllabi from other faculty to generate ideas for your own document. It also is useful for instructors to articulate for themselves what is important in the course. Ideally, from a student's perspective, the syllabus should provide some general insight on the instructor's methods and philosophy, not to mention what kinds of work will be expected. A good syllabus should contain the following elements (excerpts from two sample syllabi are provided in the appendix).

Course Description and Learning Objectives

The course description is usually a blurb of no more than a few sentences that encapsulates the topics for the course. This often is followed by the learning objectives or outcomes for students. Because the objectives usually focus on what the successful student should be able to do or know, they are important not only in clarifying expectations for students and their performance but also in providing instructors with specific goals for which they can align their activities. If the college has not determined the objectives, this should be one of the instructor's first tasks, because this will help with establishing a framework for the course. Cross and Angelo (1988) asserted that instructors should examine their goals and include objectives and activities that will accomplish them; to this end, instructors can use a tool such as the Teaching Goals Inventory. Instructors should also use verbs identified in Bloom's taxonomy of educational objectives (1956); they can assist an instructor in representing a range of thinking skills within the objectives.

Teaching Methods and Learning Activities

The next step in developing the syllabus is to reflect on the teaching and learning activities that will help students achieve the desired objectives. Activities should be varied and selected specifically to facilitate learning. A good starting point is to take each objective in a course and envision the teaching methods and learning activities for accomplishing it. For instance, an objective that deals with understanding historical context might be met through mini-lecture, small group discussion, game or quiz, guest speaker, or a Web site research assignment. An objective that deals with analyzing or evaluating different techniques in a content area might be met through individual case studies, small-group problem solving, simulations, experiments, peer teaching, or writing assignments. It is worthwhile to plan several activities or methods to address each objective, paying attention to different learning styles or preferences. In the syllabus itself, an instructor may provide only the general topic and highlights for each class, choosing to be more expansive on the assignments that follow the session. Teaching methods and learning activities are treated in greater detail by the instructor in the lesson plan.

Assessment and Evaluation Strategies and Criteria

Assessment has become a national priority and is a critical element in the design of any instructional program. Students need frequent and accurate feedback on how well they are doing. Just as it is important to use a variety of teaching and learning activities, it is advisable to use a variety of assessment and evaluation strategies. Classroom assessment techniques (Cross & Angelo, 1988) include students' ungraded responses to what they know or how they feel about a lesson, a lecture, or another teaching method. They are an invaluable source of instructional feedback that help to shape how we approach the balance of the course. Formal evaluation methods are graded and often include quizzes, exams, papers, presentations, and projects; these, too, offer instructors valuable information on students' skills and competencies. It is important to vary evaluations, both in the methods and the timing. If students are evaluated solely on the basis of written tests, what is the effect on students who perform best through communicating orally? If 90% of a student's grade is based on an evaluation that takes place in the last week of class, what message is conveyed to students about the work done throughout the semester?

> *If students are evaluated solely on the basis of written tests, what is the effect on students who perform best through communicating orally? If 90% of a student's grade is based on an evaluation that takes place in the last week of class, what message is conveyed to students about the work done throughout the semester?*

Letter-Grade Criteria

In addition to describing how a student will be evaluated, some colleges require instructors to articulate their letter-grade criteria. Required or not, it is simply good practice. When developing criteria, instructors should ask themselves what they will look for in order to determine that students have successfully met the objectives. In addition, the criteria should be developed such that achieving the objectives to the *A* level requires exceptional performance. When the criteria are shared with the class in the first session, it provides students with clear expectations for accomplishing the objectives. Some community colleges allow students to choose a pass/fail approach to their courses. This may be appealing to lifelong learners or students in developmental or elective courses.

Develop a Lesson Plan

A lesson plan is an even more extensive and detailed breakdown of the semester by class session. This is a major piece of work for instructors and represents a great deal of planning. Instructors outline the topics for each class session, identify which learning objectives are being addressed, articulate the methods that will be used in the class, and explain how the learning will be assessed or evaluated. Many instructors also include their lecture notes, directions for activities, topics and questions for discussion, and goals they want to achieve. This is not a document that is given out to students, but rather an internal planning tool for the instructor. Although it takes time to develop this kind of plan, its benefits to the teaching–learning process are immense. Instructors can visualize the semester as a whole, making sure they have addressed different learning styles in their methods, integrated classroom assessments into their activities, prepared students for formal evaluation, scheduled homework and other assignments in a timely and meaningful manner, and built in opportunities for variety and relevance in learning. Many instructors believe that the more work they do in preparing for their course, the freer they can be in the classroom to find teachable moments.

Rather than discouraging spontaneity in the classroom, the planning process provides the framework or conditions for learning and allows instructors the freedom to listen, provide connections, and teach. In fact, some instructors create their lesson plan—paradoxically perhaps—so they do not have to use it.

Lesson plans vary widely by instructor. Some instructors create a brief outline of teaching and learning activities for each class session and include only the necessary materials and time estimates for tasks. Other instructors specify the essential objectives being addressed in each session and even include a sample script or important talking points they want to convey to students during the class. Just as there is no one right way to learn, there is no one right way to teach. That said, the more work instructors do to visualize their course's architecture—what students will learn and how they will learn it—the more inviting and clear it will be to students. Rather than discouraging spontaneity in the classroom, the planning process provides the framework or conditions for learning and allows instructors the freedom to listen, provide connections, and teach. In fact, some instructors create their lesson plan—paradoxically perhaps—so they do not have to use it. They may refer to it at times, but it is more of a springboard for their work in the classroom. A sample lesson plan appears in the appendix.

Integrate Technology Into Courses

In response to demand for improved access, scheduling flexibility, and experience with current technologies, most community colleges now offer courses and programs through distance learning. Public two-year institutions in 2000–01 had the greatest number of enrollments in distance education, totaling almost half a million, according to the National Center for Educational Statistics (Waits & Lewis, 2003). The most common delivery methods were through Internet and video technologies. Because continued growth is expected in the next five years, the effectiveness of distance education compared with traditional classroom instruction has been the subject of sustained inquiry. Research has consistently shown that good teaching practices, regardless of the delivery method, have the greatest impact on student outcomes; when courses make clear connections between learning outcomes and assessment and incorporate good instructional design, distance learning is as effective as classroom-based instruction (Johnson & Benson, 2003).

Incorporate technological resources as you would other resources. Community colleges are committed to offering students the opportunity to learn the necessary skills to succeed in today's world, and there are many ways that we as instructors can make effective use of technology to support teaching and learning. These are important whether we are teaching online or in a traditional classroom. For many instructors, this means integrating relevant and engaging Web sites into their course materials. The Internet has certainly opened the floodgates to materials that instructors and students did not have access to before. However, access alone is not enough; instructors have a responsibility to teach students how to navigate resources, sift through information, make meaning from disparate pieces, and then integrate all of this into a way of thinking and being in the world. We cannot afford to treat Internet resources, any more than printed material, with passivity. If we do not employ active learning strategies to develop their critical thinking and literacy skills, students will not be freed by their access to a wealth of information but paralyzed by it.

Another tool many instructors use is a course management system such as Blackboard or WebCT—Internet portals that integrate and individualize Web-based tools and resources for both instructors and students. These systems and other course management software allow instructors teaching online or in traditional classrooms to post relevant materials in one place where all students can easily find them, set up links to specific Web sites, create groups for online assignments, and return work to students electronically with individualized feedback. Most important, however, course management systems allow instructors to foster a student's sense of community and voice through developing asynchronous discussion forums, where students respond to each other and the instructor through writing. In the discussion forum, students craft responses to instructors' questions, develop questions of their own, and address each other's ideas and speculations. This can have a profound impact on learning when used purposefully by instructors. This technology is a tool that can go far in helping us transform students from passive to active, from bored to engaged, and from bystanders to learners.

In 1996 Chickering and Ehrmann published "Implementing the Seven Principles: Technology as Lever" as a follow-up to Chickering and Gamson's (1987) "Seven Principles for Good Practice in Undergraduate Education." It was Chickering and Ehrmann's (1996) assertion that "if the power of new technologies is to be fully realized, they should be employed in ways consistent with" the practices of good teaching (p. 3). Whether we are teaching in an online, hybrid, or bricks-and-mortar classroom, it is our responsibility as educators to use all our resources in service to the principles of good teaching.

Build Community in the First Weeks of Class

The first weeks of class are an important time for both instructors and students. It is vital to set norms, articulate expectations, develop rapport, and establish what students know about the subject. On the student's part, beginning a class can be a risky and intimidating process. Students may feel isolated and ill at ease. They may imagine that everyone knows more than they do about a subject, and even the most excited and confident student may entertain thoughts of dropping the course at the slightest hint of failure or difficulty. There are, however, ways of building students' interest and commitment at the beginning of the semester.

Get to Know the Students
One way of developing rapport is to make time early in the semester to get to know the students. After all, students want to be seen as individuals and want to feel that instructors care about them as people. Most students also want to find out about their instructors—they want to know what kinds of people we are and how we are likely to behave in the classroom. In addition, the more we can do to encourage students to learn about each other, the better their collaborative work is likely to be later on. Some strategies for developing this rapport in the first weeks include the following.

■ Learn students' names. Have students create name placards to place in front of themselves for the first few weeks of class. Not only does this help instructors, but it also helps other students. Students could also introduce themselves verbally and tell a little bit about why they are taking a course.

■ Ask students to write about themselves. This writing could take the form of a letter or notes on an index card. Some of the questions that we might ask include the following. Why are you taking the class? What do you want to get from the experience? What kinds of questions do you have about the course? How do you learn best? Is there something you want me to know about yourself? In addition, we might assign students to write about their knowledge of or experience with the subject. For instance, students might write a short autobiography of themselves as writers or political beings or consumers.

■ Create an icebreaker activity that emphasizes getting to know each other. One such activity is human bingo, whereby students must sign off on squares that describe something they have experience doing or being (e.g., lived outside the United States, has more than three siblings, plays a musical instrument). When a student has five signatures in a typical bingo pattern, she or he says so and the game is finished. As a result of this kind of activity, students learn about each other and begin the semester on a positive note. The bingo squares can also be tailored to relate to a specific field or area of content in order to make the game more course-specific. In other words, a computer instructor might create a bingo game built around common terms (mouse, hard drive, file) and then call out definitions or clues. Working in small groups, students try to match the definitions to the terms on their bingo square. This exercise is a useful way for instructors to assess students' knowledge of the subject early on in the semester.

■ Have students interview each other. Give students an opportunity to work with another person in the class. Pairs can interview each other and then introduce their partners to the class at large. Instructors might suggest questions that are related to being in college but also questions that are connected to the content of the course.

■ Have students complete a questionnaire that explores their knowledge of the subject. A business instructor might ask: "What do you think are the most important qualities an employer wants in a new hire?" or "Imagine that you could design the perfect leader, what qualities or skills would you give him or her?" A psychology instructor might ask: "What words come to mind when you think of the term 'counseling'?" The questions can serve to pique students' interest about upcoming attractions in the course, and students' responses provide instructors with important feedback on what students know or think they know about the course. Ausubel (cited in Cross & Angelo, 1988) stated that "the most important single factor influencing learning is what the learner already knows" (p. 18).

Introduce the Subject

In the first class, it is vital to introduce at least one compelling and interesting aspect of the subject. It will not always be apparent to students what they are going to learn in the course, even with a syllabus right in front of them. Therefore, the instructor needs to introduce the subject (and upcoming highlights in the course) with enthusiasm, involving students in the process. Some ideas for accomplishing this are as follows.

In the first class, it is vital to introduce at least one compelling and interesting aspect of the subject. It will not always be apparent to students what they are going to learn in the course, even with a syllabus right in front of them.

■ Do a small-group activity. Break students into small groups and ask them to brainstorm on topics related to the subject. A literature instructor might ask students to think about their most memorable characters in literature and describe what makes them so.

■ Present a short excerpt of a video or audiotape. A world history instructor might show a video excerpt of a reenactment or scene and ask students to take notes on everything they notice about the style of dress, the language, the tools or weapons that are used, and the relationships between characters. Afterwards, the class could break for small-group discussions or talk as a whole group.

■ Present visual material. A writing instructor might present an array of photographs or paintings, asking students to choose one and write about the scene from the subject's perspective. A business instructor might present sample product logos and ask students to develop a list of associations or strengths and weaknesses.

■ Introduce a problem or case study. Even if students are not ready to solve the problem, it will get them engaged in the process. In addition, students can brainstorm on aspects of solving it; for instance, students in a statistics class could weigh in on defining the problem and what information or tools are needed to solve it. At the end of the semester, the statistics instructor might introduce the problem again as to drive home how much students have learned in the course.

Articulate Expectations and Develop Classroom Norms

In the first weeks of class, students look to instructors to set their expectations on a variety of issues, including how much study or homework time is needed, how important it is to arrive on time to class and to be prompt with assignments, and how students should relate to each other during discussion and other interactions. Students may even wonder what they should call instructors and what the appropriate protocol is for leaving the class to use the restroom. Instructors can anticipate a lot of these questions when they go over the syllabus with students, but they may also want to do the following.

■ Ask students to anonymously write down questions about the class on index cards, which can then be collected, read aloud, and answered.

■ Involve students in developing some classroom rules or norms. Ask each small group in the class to develop five rules that will help foster a supportive learning environment for everyone. Put these on the board, looking for opportunities to achieve consensus. Adults, especially, feel more ownership in a course when they have been consulted.

■ Create a list of assumptions for students in the class. This list could be a way for instructors to articulate in writing their expectations and might include things like: "I assume all students will call me and leave a message when they are not going to be in class, unless there is an emergency." After this list is disseminated, ask students to work in small groups to develop assumptions they have for the instructor. The discussion that follows could help to alleviate future misunderstandings and create a more satisfactory experience for all.

In addition to these suggestions, instructors may want to formulate strategies for dealing with common classroom problems before they occur. For example, late or missing assignments are a perennial problem for instructors everywhere, and community colleges are no exception. Not only is it useful to go over the expectations around deadlines and the consequences for submitting late work, it is equally important to imagine how expectations or policies will be challenged by students. What will you do if a student weaves a tale of woe as a reason for not completing the assignment? And how will you respond to a student who submits nothing throughout the first half of the semester, but then turns up in class with all the missing work? These kinds of situations can catch instructors off-guard. By imagining the ways your expectations might be challenged, you can decide whether modifications or caveats are needed. In addition, you can respond to students' crises or situations with empathy, because you will not be worrying so much about what to do. Even when a student's dilemma does catch us by surprise, rarely do we need to respond with an immediate answer. Taking time to consider the situation and its implications may be the best response of all.

Use Small Groups Effectively

It is vitally important in the first sessions to foster a sense of community. A healthy classroom learning community enables students to think boldly, take risks, and celebrate the diversity of individuals. Of course, a number of techniques can be employed to do this, but one of the most effective methods for developing a student's sense of ownership of a course is through the use of small groups. Small groups work well in classrooms because they

- get all students actively participating in the work

- engage quieter students who might be less willing to speak out in a large group

- offer students a safer environment to test out their ideas

- encourage students to work collaboratively, rather than competitively

- foster student leadership opportunities, and these can change according to the topic and the group's membership, so that there is more diversity in the leaders

- develop students' critical thinking and speaking skills

- allow students to own aspects of the course, the subject, and the process of learning

- offer instructors the opportunity to assess how well students understand the material by watching them work

- allow instructors to give direct and immediate feedback, whether groups are struggling or thinking in creative and original ways

Small-group sessions can be effective for brainstorming, problem-solving, or analyzing material. The most effective ways to design and implement small-group activities are as follows.

- Use them regularly. Many instructors break the class into small groups at least once every session, sometimes more. Students come to understand the role of the small group and get right to work.

- Have a prepared task, problem, or question for students to tackle. Some instructors give all small groups the same problem and then use the discussion that follows as a way of illustrating the range in thinking. Other instructors give each group their own question or problem, asking groups to then present or teach their findings to the rest of the class.

■ Assign a variety of tasks to groups. Experimenting with different tasks or problems will allow students to develop and refine their skills. Variety will also keep students engaged in the activities.

■ Establish groups of three to six students. Of course, students can and should work in pairs on certain activities, but for the purposes of a small-group activity, there should be a minimum of three students. Groups of more than six students may be too large for all students to participate freely.

■ Change the membership of the groups, but not so often as to create discord. Some instructors might assign groups to work as consultants for each other on major projects. In this case, it might be best to have students stay in the same group for this work. However, for most purposes, membership in a small group could change regularly. The reward for changing groups is that students get to work with different peers and develop broader skills.

■ Give students the opportunity to form their own groups on occasion. Although it may serve an instructor's purpose to arrange the membership of small groups, it is good to occasionally give students the freedom and flexibility to choose their working partners.

■ Vary students' responsibilities or roles in groups. Sometimes assign the group facilitators, recorders, and presenters, and at other times allow groups to assign these roles themselves.

Finally, it is a good idea to ask students to assess their own learning in the small groups. What roles did they play? How did the group work to solve its task or explore its topic? Golding and Weimer (2004) explored what happens when students understand certain principles but fail to apply them in the group setting. By reflecting deliberately on the processes of learning, not just the products, students can better transform theory into practice.

Use Classroom Assessment Techniques

In the first weeks, it is important to assess how the class is going from the student perspective. This can be done simply through classroom assessment techniques (Cross & Angelo, 1988), in which the instructor asks for student feedback on a specific or general topic. Not only do assessments help instructors to see the course from another perspective, but also a good assessment also can act as a powerful tool for learning. In addition, they let students know that instructors care about their opinions. Some common assessment techniques used by instructors in the classroom are as follows.

■ The one-minute paper. Cross and Angelo (1988) suggested ending class periods by having each student do a one-minute paper, consisting of two questions: What is the most significant thing you learned in this session? What is the most significant question you have about today's lesson? Anonymous responses encourage candor.

■ Word associations. Some instructors ask students to write (anonymously) the adjectives that best describe how they feel about the week's in-class activities or homework assignments. Of course, when we undertake an exercise like this, we might elicit words such as *interested* and *excited*; we could also get words like *bored* or *confused*. However risky this might be from our perspective, it is helpful to know what students are thinking. In addition, this kind of assessment forces students to name their feelings and take ownership of them.

■ Index-card feedback. Other instructors take a similar approach using index cards. At the end of class, each student is asked anonymously: What was the most important thing you learned in this class? What did we discuss that you do not understand? What activities would help you to learn this subject? At the beginning of the next class, the instructor shares the results of the previous week's index card assessment and makes adjustments as appropriate.

■ Punctuated lectures. Some instructors use punctuated lectures (Cross & Angelo, 1988), pausing after ten minutes and asking students to take a minute or two to write down one important idea or fact presented in that part of the lecture. Students then volunteer to share their responses. It is not uncommon to find that they missed the most important points in the lecture and that a reinforcement of those points is needed. This exercise also turns what could be a passive activity into an active learning one.

■ Reflective opportunities. Besides asking students to give feedback on the class or what they know from a lecture, instructors also can ask students to reflect on their learning process. For example, many instructors follow a small-group activity with a short assessment asking students to reflect on their contribution to the group. Instructors can connect assessment to their assignments or exams by asking students to reflect on what was most challenging or rewarding about the assignment, what they would do differently if they had the chance, and what lesson(s) they might draw from completing such an assignment. Instructors might also finish an assignment or activity by asking students to choose an image that represents some aspect of the topic that is most meaningful to them.

Classroom assessment techniques can be powerful ways to improve learning and performance, regardless of whether the feedback comes from instructors or from students. We all need feedback if we are to be most effective in our teaching and learning. Assessment techniques can be built into the flow of regular activities, and they can enliven and energize the course. Whichever of these techniques we use, assessments should not be graded. Students must feel free to respond spontaneously and honestly. The reason for doing the assessment should be explained to students and it should be clear how the information gained could benefit all.

Cross and Angelo (1988) suggested ending class periods by having each student do a one-minute paper, consisting of two questions: What is the most significant thing you learned in this session? What is the most significant question you have about today's lesson?

Keep Learners Engaged

Instructors spend most of their time in the classroom covering the material and teaching students. These two processes may or may not happen at the same time. In fact, we can cover the course content and yet not teach students; conversely, we can teach students while ignoring the content. However, a critical element in these processes is missing: learning. Because learning begins when attention is gained and ends when attention is lost, the most important task for instructors during most of the course may be keeping students engaged. Of course, we can do this in various ways: we can organize our content effectively, use active learning strategies, design assignments that have meaning and interest, assess how students are learning, be responsive in our teaching, and give students valuable and timely feedback.

Organize Content for Successful Learning

Simply stated, we can do a lot to make our content accessible to students if we use a variety of instructional methods and provide experiences that touch on many different learning styles. Much of what we do depends on the subject and our own personal teaching style. However, it also is important to work beyond our teaching preferences, to stretch ourselves in the same way we ask students to. As a result, many of us can benefit from some kind of framework for preparing course activities. The following sequence is adapted from two tested approaches to instructional design: mastery learning and expository teaching. Instructors from a variety of disciplines have successfully adapted this approach for their own purposes.

Much of what we do depends on the subject and our own personal teaching style. However, it also is important to work beyond our teaching preferences, to stretch ourselves in the same way we ask students to.

■ Take the course objectives and determine which objective(s) or sub-parts of an objective will be learned in a particular class session or lesson. Translate these desired outcomes into an overall, general goal for the session or for a specific lesson.

■ Present the class with an overview of the content to be learned in each session. This statement can be delivered simply as a mini-lecture or presented in a short reading passage, a cartoon, a series of slides, a tape recording, or a demonstration. It should be relatively short and as simple as possible. This step serves as an advance organizer for the lesson and provides the students with an anchor for the more specific, detailed elements to follow.

■ Through a question-and-answer session, determine the degree to which the students catch on to the organizing concept. Once again, this is classroom assessment. If some students do not understand it, you will have to provide further explanation. McKeachie (1978) reminds us that learners can create new knowledge only out of what is already in their heads. In other words, there has to be some match between the concept being presented and the conceptual readiness of students.

■ Introduce the more detailed aspects of the subject matter. This can be done through discussion, active learning exercises, demonstrations, audiovisuals, or whatever is appropriate. If possible, give the students clues about the relative importance of each point or piece of information. Always reinforce the connection between the specifics and the organizing concept.

■ The learning can then be strengthened using small groups to discuss related questions or solve problems. Large-group integration of small-group results can further consolidate the learning for students.

- Finish the lesson or session with some type of evaluation procedure or classroom assessment technique. It can be an informal discussion or a brief quiz. Some instructors like to have small groups solve problems with the material. Students might write test or discussion questions. Their questions often reveal as much about their thoughts and understanding as their answers do, and they further reinforce the skills of critical thinking. Additional readings or opportunities for students to apply the knowledge can be assigned as homework.

Use Active Learning Strategies

In many traditional college classrooms, lecture is the primary mode of teaching, despite the fact that research conducted by the National Training Laboratories (n.d.) reports an average retention rate of only about 5% for information delivered in lecture form. Some instructors still believe that lecture is the quickest and most efficient way to deliver information. However, this belief assumes that learning is primarily information-gathering rather than knowledge-building. If we want our students to develop critical thinking and writing skills, we must move beyond the image of the passive learner. Because students prefer, on the whole, to interact with other students, the instructor, and the course material, it makes sense for us to use strategies that promote learning and make it enjoyable.

Active learning strategies do just this; they engage students in the learning process, especially the higher-order skills of analysis and synthesis. Very simply, they involve students in doing things and thinking about the things they are doing. There are numerous possibilities for activities that support this type of learning, including the following

- Break up a lecture. Ask students to articulate the five most important points of the lecture, create examples that support the lecture, or develop a problem or question that is connected to the lecture. They may do this in writing or in small-group discussion.

- Assign in-class writing. Students can respond to questions or topics individually in writing and then share their responses in pairs or small groups. When writing precedes discussion, students have more investment in the dialogue that takes place. In-class writing can also help students to make connections. Students can be asked to find metaphors for new material; for instance, students might be asked to fill in the blanks on statements such as the following. "What I learned today reminds me of _____ because _____." "I want to bring to the study of _____ the skills I have in _____, in that I learn how to _____ and _____." A psychology student might answer the second statement with: "I want to bring to the study of human personality the skills I have in singing, in that I learn how to better read people and find harmony in our interactions." When students make connections between new material and things they already know, there is a much better chance they will retain and integrate the new learning.

- Assign problems to solve. Theories and principles can be reinforced by asking students to apply their skills to solving problems, in the form of case studies, role-playing, or examples. Adult students especially enjoy seeing the practical aspects of knowledge. In addition, working in this way helps students to build critical thinking skills.

- Facilitate peer teaching. Students can collaborate in groups to organize small amounts of material into lessons. This is an effective follow-up to a lecture or reading assignment. Small groups take responsibility for a certain aspect of the material and develop a quiz, song, visual illustration, or other learning tool. Each group then teaches its lesson to the class.

- Play games. Some instructors use games as a way of reviewing large chunks of material before an exam. Games can be engaging, and they promote retention; they also can provide a fun release for the class, especially if students are stressed. Instructors may create their own versions of many popular quiz games. It is important, however, to have a clear sense of the goal in using games. For instance, most instructors are careful to avoid putting students in uncomfortable situations. Instead, students may be arranged in small groups or teams to answer questions, so that everyone is offered an opportunity to contribute, and the goal is clearly articulated.

Of course, active learning is a useful method in more than the traditional classroom. Online instructors can also easily create an active learning environment. To begin with, instructors can design the types of questions that create active learning in the discussion forum; for example, learners can be required to analyze, synthesize, compare and contrast, or reflect about specific content or issues in the course. When possible, students should be encouraged to apply their learning through the use of ancillary Web sites and other appropriate technology; for example, instructors can introduce students to excellent, scholarly Web sites where learners engage in virtual learning. Finally, instructors themselves can engage in active learning as a member of the online class.

Design Assignments That Work

It is frustrating when assignments fail—when students are confused or bored and when the work that is turned in does not match our expectations. Many factors can contribute to an assignment that falls flat, and regular classroom assessment can provide an instructor with some of these. A good assignment has a clear purpose that is directly related to accomplishing the course objectives. That purpose is articulated to students. The assignment is word processed, copied, and disseminated to students. Instructors explain when the assignment is due, how long it should take, and how it will be used or addressed in class. Students should also know the consequences of failing to complete the assignment. Tips for designing effective assignments include the following.

- When creating an assignment, think about how it relates to the learning objectives for the course. What are the goals for the assignment? How will learning be evaluated with regard to this assignment?

- Try to see the connections between parts of the subject and the methods, and then try to articulate these connections to students. A good course feels integrated and seamless even though it may be made up of many different pieces.

- Make expectations explicit and clear. Put assumptions into writing. After creating an assignment, spend time envisioning what a successful product would look like. Think of how that vision can be conveyed to students. Are there examples? Can you describe what you want from students?

- Think about all the possible questions students might have (e.g., what kinds of topics would be acceptable?). The better we are at articulating our expectations, the more likely students are to submit work that meets them.

- Balance the methods for evaluating students. If the bulk of a student's grade rests on one assignment, what message is being conveyed about the other parts of the course?

- Balance the timing of evaluation methods. Do not leave everything until the end of the semester. This creates a lot of pressure for students and emphasizes the products of a student's learning rather than the process.

- Aim for balance with regard to evaluation and assessment. Create ways of assessing students' progress without grading them. This will help to keep students on track and moving forward.

- Students do better on assignments that are relevant and engaging. Give students choices whenever possible. Let them decide their own topic for a paper, or let them choose among assignments. One student might write a short paper while another builds a model and presents it to the class.

- Even if all students complete the same assignment, they can still be involved in the process: brainstorming steps to complete the assignment, thinking about how it should be evaluated, determining possible approaches to the assignment.

Create Quizzes, Tests, and Exams

Some students clearly dislike tests. However, this feeling may result from taking tests that have been poorly designed, that trick students into making mistakes, and that seem to outweigh all other work produced in the course. Davis (1993) has argued that tests can be powerful tools in that they evaluate learning, motivate and provide structure for students, assess how well material is being presented, and enhance learning by providing students with important feedback.

Tests should be seen as a way of capturing what students do know, not what they do not.

It is perhaps most important to remember that just as instructors should provide variety in teaching and evaluation methods, they also should provide variety in their tests. To begin with, tests should be seen as a way of capturing what students do know, not what they do not. Although it is tempting to create one kind of test format and use it consistently throughout a semester, students will benefit more from being exposed to different formats. This gives all learners an equal chance at success, and it encourages instructors to find the best format for different material and goals. Whatever test you use, discuss it when it is returned to students. Discussion provides feedback and reinforcement of learning. Do not, of course, embarrass an individual by discussing his or her wrong answer unless the student raises the issue.

TIPS FOR CREATING QUIZZES, TESTS, AND EXAMS

- Spend time creating them. Preparing a meaningful exam can take a lot of effort, but it is worth it in the long run. Students appreciate the opportunity to reflect on their learning. When creating a test, think carefully about what students need to know to do well on it. Make sure students have been adequately prepared by assignments and class work. Do not introduce new material or concepts. Make sure that questions or tasks are clear and unambiguous. It is also a good idea to let students know how sections or parts weigh in relation to the whole test. This helps students to manage their time most effectively, an important skill even in take-home tests.

- Address different levels of learning. Use a tool such as Bloom's (1956) taxonomy of educational objectives to make sure that questions or tasks are not focused on one level. Some tests will address learning at the knowledge or first level and neglect the higher level skills associated with comprehension, application, analysis, synthesis, and evaluation. However, it is precisely these higher-level skills that we want to encourage in students.

■ Create an effective structure. It often is better, in a test with different sections or parts, to place easier questions first. These might be questions related to the knowledge or comprehension levels in Bloom's taxonomy and that begin with the verbs *list, cite, match, identify, name, define,* or *calculate.* By placing easier questions or tasks first, you give students an opportunity to build their confidence and success before tackling some of the more challenging parts. A well-constructed test allows students to recall information, reinforce the learning, reorganize their thoughts, and use higher-level thinking.

■ Create opportunities for reflection and meaning. Exams should offer students the chance to synthesize and reflect on their learning. In order for students to make connections between past experiences and new knowledge or skills, instructors must create at least some questions that can be answered in more than one way. This not only encourages students to think deeply about the material, but also it may help prevent academic dishonesty.

■ Give students some choices. One of the best strategies for showing students that an exam is intended to assess what they know is to offer them some choice in the questions they answer. For example, one section of an exam might ask students to choose five quotes (out of a bank of ten), identify the speakers, provide a context, and argue the merits. Another section might ask students to choose one essay question or topic and write a response. This kind of structure sends a message to students that instructors are not trying to trick them but discover what they really have to say.

■ Involve students in the test-making process. This promotes active learning and enhances students' critical thinking skills. Students may be divided into small groups and given responsibility to create a specific number of questions on the material. Instructors assign each group a different part of the material or different types of questions (multiple choice, true/false, essay). All groups develop questions and possible answers. Instructors monitor the process and make copies of each group's work. The class receives these copies and can use them in the study process. Instructors commit to using a certain number of questions on the exam, although they may be altered in some way. This activity promotes ownership in the course for students; they learn a great deal from composing questions and imagining both right and wrong answers. Because this happens in the small group setting, students' knowledge and skill with the material is also enhanced. Finally, student test-makers tend to design harder tests than do instructors yet rarely complain about the test when it is time to take it. Daloz (1986) said that "good teachers ought to help students learn not simply to answer questions but to ask better ones themselves" (p. 229).

■ Think about when to administer a test. Timing is everything when giving a test. It is best to give it when students are fresh but have had an opportunity to settle into the class. If the test is given at the end of a long class, students may feel anxious and tired by the time they approach the exam. If it is given at the very beginning of a class, students who are late may be a distraction for others. Also, students may not have settled into the business of the class and may still be thinking of their jobs or families, whatever preceded their coming to class. It is also not a good idea to introduce new material before an exam because it can confuse students. At the same time, many instructors are reluctant to do a review directly before the exam because this can feel like prepping. It may be best to do a type of icebreaker exercise that relates to the material of the test but does not review it, and then administer the exam. This gets students in a learning frame of mind.

TYPES OF QUESTIONS TO USE Tests are most useful when they are used throughout the course. Frequent quizzes can help instructors monitor the pulse of the class and individual students. They also can increase the efficiency of learning. In addition, when tests are varied in the type of questions they ask, they can provide students with additional skills and enrich understanding.

■ Essay questions are effective in assessing the mastery of higher-order objectives. Essays gives students the opportunity to interpret material, generalize about it, and evaluate it. Remember, although essay questions are easier to construct, they are more difficult and time-consuming to correct. Let students know what they are looking for: good organization, depth of analysis, use of examples, or other areas of emphasis.

■ Short-answer items are effective for moving students from straight recall and recognition skills to slightly higher levels of comprehension. Students can be asked to fill in blanks in a statement, complete a sentence, or respond to a question in a sentence or two. Short-answer items can assess whether students are picking up the important details.

■ True/false items can measure the ability to recall or comprehend large amounts of information. Be careful to make the questions of similar length and to eliminate as much ambiguity as possible. They are easy to score, but because students can get them correct by chance alone, their use should be limited. One strategy for improving the true/false quiz is to ask students to choose any number of their false statements and explain why they are not accurate or true.

■ Good multiple-choice questions are harder to develop than most other types. They can, however, measure different levels of learning from simple recall to much higher levels of comprehension. If an instructor teaches a course on a continuing basis, she or he can develop, test, and revise a few each semester until there is a good selection. The stem statement should be brief, and it should not provide clues to the correct answer. The choices for answers (a four- or five-option approach is recommended) should be carefully selected to provide one that is clearly correct and several distracters that hold some promise as being correct answers. Instructors should not include an off-the-wall distracter. It does nothing but embarrass the students who select it. Again, it may be useful to provide students with the opportunity to explain why they chose each of their answers. Not only does this allow instructors to follow students' thinking process, it can provide instructors with critical feedback on the questions many students miss.

■ Consider giving take-home exams. They do not use up valuable class time, and they allow students an extended period of time to think about their answers. Of course, take-home exams should solicit conceptual understanding of the material; the textbook and other references can be used to gather evidence to back up assertions. Do not ask questions that can be answered directly with factual information from the textbook.

Relate to Students Interpersonally

Many of us understand that our job as instructors is to help students learn a subject and develop their skills and abilities. However, students sometimes learn as much from how we relate to them as from what we try to teach them. In *Effective Teaching and Mentoring*, Daloz (1986) asserted that powerful and lasting learning can occur through the conversations and relationships that develop between instructor and student. Effective instructors "balance both a present sense of where their students are and a dream of what they can become—without allowing either to eclipse the other" (Daloz, 1986, p. 218). Palmer (1997) also emphasized the importance of the instructor–student relationship when working with faculty, although he asserted that the power of our own mentor–instructors "is in their capacity to awaken a truth within us, a truth we can reclaim years later by recalling the impact on our lives" (p. 21). Instructors can develop the interpersonal dimension in their classes by actively listening to and encouraging students.

PROMOTE ACTIVE LISTENING When instructors speak, students listen, but it is just as important for instructors to listen to students. However, listening may not be the same as active listening. Active listening can help make the student feel important and valued. When that happens, the student usually becomes more motivated to learn. Active listening starts by attending to the learner. This means physically posturing ourselves to listen: leaning forward and making eye contact. We also need to observe the student for physical clues about emotions, energy level, and motivation.

Active listening starts by attending to the learner. This means physically posturing ourselves to listen: leaning forward and making eye contact. We also need to observe the student for physical clues about emotions, energy level, and motivation.

Responding is the key to the whole active-listening process. A response technique that is especially effective for instructors is paraphrasing. Paraphrasing is a way to connect with the learner. "Beth, I hear you saying that every time you get rolling on studying, something happens at home to interrupt. It also seems that you get frustrated and annoyed that you cannot keep up with the assignments." In this case the instructor is using paraphrasing to reflect back to the student her understanding of the student's concern. Regardless of the accuracy of the instructor's interpretation, it shows a deep interest in the student's comment; a strong attempt to understand is powerful medicine for the student who needs to feel listened to. It also gives the student a chance to clarify and expand on the original comment, if the paraphrase was off the mark: "That isn't quite what I meant, but . . ."

Paraphrasing also helps instructors confirm their understanding of students' comments and questions before giving advice, providing an answer, or asking other students to comment. Nothing falls quite as flat as a response based on a misunderstood statement. As instructors improve their active listening skills, their paraphrasing will address the content, the attendant feelings, and the meaning of students' remarks when appropriate. In the example above, the content had to do with the interruptions; the feelings of frustration were noted, and the student's inability to keep up was the reason for the frustration. This type of paraphrasing can put instructors in tune with the students and make all subsequent communication more effective.

OFFER REINFORCEMENT AND ENCOURAGEMENT B. F. Skinner and a host of other behaviorists have taught us that reinforced behavior tends to persist and increase; behavior that is not reinforced will eventually stop. One way to reinforce a desired behavior is through praise: "Janet, that was a good job." In this case, the praise will be effective if Janet agrees that it indeed was a good job.

Encouragement is a variation on praise as a form of reinforcement. It focuses on a particular aspect of a student's performance with more specificity: "Janet, in your paper I noticed that you support your argument with a wealth of information taken from a variety of sources." This approach appears to have great potential to nourish the student's feelings of accomplishment and worth.

In using encouragement, the instructor must watch for good work, determine what makes it good, and let the student know about it either through an oral or written comment. The specificity gives encouragement its power because it indicates that the instructor has carefully noted the student's performance and is genuinely impressed. If a student is struggling, encouragement can be based on effort. "I noticed, Mike, you put a lot of time, effort, and thought into that paper. I can already see improvement in grammar and organization."

RESPOND TO DISRUPTIVE STUDENTS Despite our best efforts to communicate positively, on occasion we might encounter students whose behavior ranges from the merely annoying to the seriously disruptive. Luckily, discipline problems are rare. Most community college students are serious about their commitment to learning, and many instructors have never encountered seriously disruptive behavior in their classes. Still, it is a good idea for instructors to familiarize themselves with their college's policies in this area and be proactive in developing their course structures and norms.

Although the single most important thing an instructor can do is to set clear expectations for classroom behavior in the first class, it often is not until a few weeks into the semester when such behavior shows itself. In addition, the behavior may begin in subtle ways, leading instructors to ignore the situation until it threatens to disrupt learning. If an instructor is faced with behavior that distracts from the learning environment, she or he should address it. The following tips can be helpful in handling the situation professionally.

- Stop teaching and talk to the condition, not the person. Instructors can describe how they feel: "I cannot teach, and the class cannot benefit from what is being said, when there are two conversations going on at the same time."

- Describe what needs to be done. An instructor might say: "Because I've already stated that Claire 'has the floor,' everyone else should avoid interrupting and wait until she is finished before making a comment."

- Avoid messages of blame, but be clear and specific. "You" messages are normally not effective, especially when things are not going right. Saying things like, "you should," "you must," "you always," "you never," or "you act like" can make the situation worse and lead to a power struggle. "I" messages are much less threatening and offensive and can even turn the situation around to something positive. An instructor might respond to a situation by saying: "I did not get a chance to hear Tom's comment" or "I have trouble staying focused on what Angela is saying when others are not paying attention to the discussion."

- Take a break to handle the situation. If the annoying or disruptive behavior continues, an instructor may have to schedule a quick break and meet privately with the student involved to explain the situation. If necessary, an instructor might coach the student on appropriate classroom behavior: However, instructors should not try to handle a serious or chronic situation alone. Instead, instructors should contact the appropriate college personnel.

- Determine what the college's expectations are in dealing with a disruptive student. Of course, it is best if you can determine this before you encounter a situation in the classroom, but if that is not possible, seek out the college's policy framework as soon as you can. In addition, ask what resources are available to help you with the situation.

Adjust the Lesson Plan and Syllabus

If instructors are using classroom assessment techniques regularly, they are likely to get feedback at some point that affects their syllabi or lesson plans. It may be that the information is also received through quizzes, homework, discussions, or questions and comments at the end of class. For example, an instructor may discover that students do not comprehend a concept they need for future work in the subject. Or students may confess that discussions are too meandering and that exercises lack continuity. Conversely, an instructor may learn in a classroom assessment that students respond positively in attitude and learning to a specific classroom activity and want to replicate it with another topic. Whatever the case, this information is extremely valuable and can warrant making adjustments to an instructor's plans. After all, good teaching is also learning.

The challenge for many of us is deciding what adjustments to make and how to handle them in ways that promote students' confidence and model flexibility. This can be different depending on when the adjustment is made and whether it affects the lesson plan (our own notebook or plan for the semester) or the syllabus (the course framework we give to students at the beginning of the semester). Some guidelines for adjusting the lesson plan and syllabus are as follows.

MAKING ADJUSTMENTS DURING CLASS

When discussions or activities work and students are enthusiastic about their learning, it is not the time to cut the lesson short, especially if this is prompted by an instructor's need to squeeze in another exercise that had been planned for the session. These moments are hard to design, and when they come, instructors should approach them as rare and blessed occurrences.

- Always plan more than what is needed. Even if we have led an activity many times, it can still work differently with each group of students. In fact, veteran instructors make small adjustments to their activities all the time to keep students engaged and learning. By having some activities in the wings, instructors can confidently move on from exercises that are not working to others that may be more successful.

- Think about the big picture. Many of us have an idea about how long it should take students to complete an exercise or test. It is quite easy from an instructional perspective to underestimate the amount of time needed in these endeavors. By the same token, we may be tempted to rush students along in the process or declare that time is up. However, if we consider the big picture, we are more likely to be patient. If the goal is learning, it does not make sense to rush students away from engaging activities in order to introduce them to new material. When giving a test, it can actually undermine student achievement to stop the process when most students in a class are still working. If only one or two students are still engaged, that is a different matter, and the instructor might offer those students a few minutes to finish up at the end of the class. If the majority of students are still working, however, it is best to be patient and cut out other activities that follow.

- Look for the teachable moment. When discussions or activities work and students are enthusiastic about their learning, it is not the time to cut the lesson short, especially if this is prompted by an instructor's need to squeeze in another exercise that had been planned for the session. These moments are hard to design, and when they come, instructors should approach them as rare and blessed occurrences.

- Change the dynamics. Sometimes we think an activity or lesson is more engaging than it is. We may go to great lengths to create relevant and meaty discussion topics only to find that when they are presented to students, no one talks. This can be quite awkward and it is tempting for instructors to fill in the dead air with their own voices. The first response to such a situation might be to wait a few moments, although silence can be deafening. Sometimes students need a little time to warm to a topic or question. If, after some time, the activity or discussion is still not working, change the dynamics. Split students into pairs or small groups and have them brainstorm on aspects of the topic. When they come back to the whole group to discuss their findings, they will be more engaged because they have had an opportunity to think about the topic and develop their ideas. For example, an instructor might begin with a question or topic on current environmental problems then ask students in small groups to consider and rank their concerns for the environment. When students gather again as a whole class, the instructor could easily use the small-group work as a bridge to a discussion on larger themes.

■ If all else fails, take a break. If things are not working in a class, rather than trying to push through the difficulty or low energy, it may be a good idea to take a time-out. Sometimes students just need a moment to refocus and reenergize, especially if the material of the class has been weighty or conceptually difficult. For example, an algebra instructor might find that after some time working on a particular lesson with formulas, students need a break before transitioning to word problems. This is also true if the subject is emotionally difficult. A human services instructor teaching on the topic of child abuse might schedule a number of breaks during the class to give students some additional time to deal with the material.

MAKING ADJUSTMENTS BETWEEN CLASSES

■ Look to the class before and the class ahead. Because things happen in the real world of the classroom that we did not anticipate or plan for, we often need to change or alter our lessons accordingly. If we were not able to teach an important concept in the last class, we may need to squeeze it into the next one. Conversely, if we found ourselves with extra time and proceeded with the lesson plan, we may need to create a new activity. Most important in this process, we want to be sure that we have continuity from week to week. This is why it is a good idea to keep at least three classes always in mind: the last one, the present one, and the next one.

If it becomes apparent that students are confused by a concept or principle, do not come to the next class prepared to spend more time using the same methods. Think about how the material can be presented differently.

■ Assess learning. The assignments or quizzes that students turn in at the end of class can be helpful for thinking about the next session. If most students missed the key questions on a test, it may be time to reevaluate how those questions are phrased so that future quizzes can be more effective. It may also be the time to make sure that content is covered in enough detail.

■ Do not teach more, teach differently. If it becomes apparent that students are confused by a concept or principle, do not come to the next class prepared to spend more time using the same methods. Think about how the material can be presented differently. Also complete the present lesson before moving on to new concepts. Take, for instance, an anatomy and physiology instructor who introduces the digestive system in the class, expecting that students will easily grasp the process. But it becomes apparent during discussion that students are confused. The instructor tries to clarify, but students are still struggling with the material by the time the class has ended. At the beginning of the next class, the instructor acknowledges the confusion and splits the class into small groups. Each group is given a set of art supplies to use in creating a model of the digestive system and must then explain how it works. In this scenario, the instructor conveys to students that their mastery of the concepts is important.

■ Assess student dynamics. If a class is planned with enough active-learning exercises, instructors are free to observe students at work independently and in groups. The information from these observations can be instrumental in planning future groups. If a student is struggling with material, he or she might be paired with a student who has a good grasp of the content. Also, instructors might notice that certain students tend to dominate discussions. These students can be arranged in one group, leaving quieter students to a group of their own.

- Gauge the effectiveness of homework. Although it can be problematic when instructors alter homework assignments, it is important to assess how effective the homework is, how much time students spend doing it, and how consistently it is completed. If students are truly buried in homework, they may feel unable to keep up and, therefore, that homework is fruitless. A good rule of thumb is that assignments should take one to three hours for every hour of class time. Of course, instructors often underestimate the amount of time it takes students to complete assignments, so it is a good idea to assess the whole process regularly. Because homework is listed on the syllabus, it is important to make these changes carefully, or students will become confused or dispirited.

ADJUSTING THE SYLLABUS

- Do not change the syllabus each week. The syllabus promises the general framework of topics and assignments for the semester. When this is altered frequently, students may distrust the process and perceive the course to be unfocused or confusing. Adult students especially appreciate the concrete aspects of the syllabus and may plan their time and energy accordingly. A good general rule is to change the syllabus no more than once or twice during a semester.

- It is easier to take things off than put them on. Sometimes adjustments to the syllabus need not result in a whole new syllabus. For students, it is easier to take off a future assignment than to decide at the last minute on an additional one. Some instructors handle the flexibility around assignments by building a space for additional assignments into the syllabus. After each week's assignments, there may be a space for "other homework," with a line or box for students to fill in as needed.

- Clearly indicate that the syllabus is a revision. When it is necessary to revise a syllabus dramatically, resulting in a new document, make sure students understand which version is the latest. Instructors can label the top with "Revision" and date it. Instructors might also copy it in a different color to reinforce the shift. It is a good idea to post the revised syllabus on the instructor's Web page, so students can always find the correct information on assignments.

- Explain why the syllabus is being changed. Instructors need to articulate their reasons to students, and these should be connected to learning. For example, an instructor might explain that she is concerned that students may not be grasping some key concepts and, therefore, she is changing the syllabus to allow the class a little more time to explore the concepts through group work or case studies. In order to make time for this work, she has dropped a homework assignment that does not relate to the project.

- Change the syllabus only when it really is needed. An instructor's lesson plan may change frequently, but it is not necessary to change the syllabus every time this happens. Many of these changes will not be apparent to students. The syllabus usually does not provide a great amount of detail on each class session. It should be updated only if dates or assignments change in a meaningful and substantive way.

As most of us know, teaching is a skill that involves intuition and flexibility. In our effort to keep students engaged and learning, we may be tempted to change direction regularly. However, as important as it is for us to be flexible in our teaching, it is also critical to recognize that students do get anxious at certain points in a semester. Sometimes this is a result of not seeing the whole picture. Sometimes this is a result of the way students approach change in general. In any case, rather than implementing large or constant changes to our courses, it may be more effective to enact small adjustments and stay steady in our belief that things will come together in the end.

Define Yourself as an Instructor

Kloss (1987), a professor of English at William Patterson College, asserted that many instructors base their teaching on certain metaphors related to the teaching–learning process, which can be problematic if we believe in these metaphors and cling to them. For example, an instructor who believes the student is "an empty vessel waiting to be filled" may teach as though she or he were pouring the course content into a passive receptacle. Instructors who operate from the "psychology laboratory" metaphor may see students as reactors to positive and negative stimuli of various sorts.

It is not that our search for metaphors is faulty, just that we need to accept that the metaphors we choose can both sustain and constrain us. If we get stuck in our own vision of ourselves, we may feel frustrated when working with students who want or need something different. In fact, our greatest challenge as instructors may be knowing which instructor to be at any moment. This does not mean we should think of ourselves as chameleons in the classroom, but we might consider, on occasion, how best to draw out the different aspects of our true selves—not an easy feat. Yet it is this kind of responsiveness that builds community and keeps learners engaged. The following are some of the metaphors others have found meaningful to describe teaching.

- Kloss (1987) has found that roles associated with coaching and playing right field work best for him; good coaches are catalysts and facilitators. Blythe and Sweet (2003) have also emphasized the abilities of a coach to make connections, break down instruction into manageable chunks, adjust strategies mid-game, develop personalized goals, and model good behavior.

- Weinstein (1999) has found inspiration in thinking about the parallels between playing jazz and teaching. He has found elements of improvisation, experimentation, surprise, and attitude that work both for the musician and the instructor.

- Marini (2000) has said that he envisions himself as a Sherpa guide when teaching because he feels that learning has striking similarities to mountain climbing. He says that learning requires a sense of adventure, perseverance, and plain hard work. Teaching then becomes a process of facilitating the climb.

- Belenky et al. (1986) suggested that the "teacher as midwife" is an appropriate role for instructors to consider. The midwife–instructor is drawing knowledge from students rather than depositing it in their heads as, for example, a "banker–teacher" might. The midwife–teacher assists the students in the birthing of their knowledge, much as the midwife and mother work together in the birthing of a child. Midwife–teachers support and assist; they see their role as fostering student growth and development. They arrange situations in which dialogue between instructor and students and among students can occur freely. This interactive process stimulates the natural tendency of everyone to grow and learn.

Besides searching for metaphors, Palmer (1999) further suggested identifying the critical moments that can occur in a course from beginning to end—the opportunities when learning "will either open up or shut down for...students" (p. 4). When we explore these moments, even in retrospect, we begin to view the teaching and learning experience, fraught with its risks and rewards, as an educational journey with all the "different starting points, routes, and destinations that journey can embrace" (Palmer, 1999, p. 5). Whatever metaphors or images we use in describing our work, it is this process of defining ourselves even in the midst of uncertainty that connects us back to the classroom and that which sustains us. And perhaps it is in our capacity as learners that we become the best models for students who, too, must navigate a changing world.

Complete a Mid-Course Evaluation of Students

At the mid-semester mark, instructors often spend time evaluating students' progress in their courses. Some colleges have specific forms, which, when completed, become part of a student's academic file. Other colleges require instructors to give a warning only when students are doing poorly enough to risk failing the course. Still other community colleges may not require any such evaluation at the mid-semester mark. Whatever the guidelines are at a college, it is useful to formally communicate with all students about their progress at the mid-course point. For one thing, it is common for students to perceive their progress differently from their instructors. In fact, students often spend a significant amount of energy trying to demystify what their instructors want from them. Taking the time to articulate a student's progress in writing can be very helpful and liberating to students. In addition, if changes are needed, there may be no better time for a student to receive this message.

Often, a mid-term evaluation gives students an indication of how well they are doing in the course on a summative basis. Although instructors should provide students with feedback on their performance all through the semester, it is important to pull together a student's performance as a whole in this type of evaluation. Students who receive detailed feedback have a better sense of where they are and what they need to do to meet the instructor's expectations. Instructors can indicate how well students have met the learning objectives and how they are performing academically. Some tips for writing narrative evaluations of students include the following:

- Give concrete examples on how well the student has met the learning objectives.

- Address any issues regarding attendance, participation, and assignment deadlines.

- Include specific areas where improvement may be needed.

- Provide encouragement in areas of strength.

- Be positive but honest and direct in communicating with the student.

- Address a student's skills or behavior, but not his or her intellect, personality, life experience, disability, race, class, age, or gender.

Students who receive detailed feedback have a better sense of where they are and what they need to do to meet the instructor's expectations.

Tips for the Last Weeks of Class

The last weeks of class can be hectic for any instructor. Usually, there is a lot to do, and instructors may worry that there is not enough time to complete all the content. Students may also be concerned; they have final exams, papers, presentations, and the inevitable separation from the course and peers to think about. Although it may be tempting to rush through the final classes in a semester, it is vital that instructors spend time in this stage of the course, allowing students to reflect, connect, and celebrate. It is also important to have strategies for dealing with last-minute crises and for evaluating final projects.

Create Opportunities for Reflection and Connection

Of course, students should spend time thinking reflectively throughout the semester. In fact, active learning requires both action and reflection in order to be useful as a teaching strategy. However, in the last classes, reflection is a way of connecting students to their original goals, the course objectives, and future learning. Some of the ways in which instructors can encourage reflection are as follows.

- Remind students of where they began. If they completed an early assessment, ask them to reflect on it and who they were when they began the course. Students also may have articulated their goals for the semester. It is a great idea to go over these at the end and ask students how they feel about those goals now. Even if students did not begin the semester with a written set of goals, instructors can ask them to think back to the beginning of the course and reflect on what they have learned and how they have changed as a result.

- Review the course objectives. In small groups, students could be assigned one or two learning objectives and asked to brainstorm the various ways in which the class met the objective. Students could also be asked to think about which objective was personally most challenging. They could describe the objectives in their own words and even rate them for importance. Then groups could present both their rating and reasoning to the rest of the class for discussion.

- Have students ask the questions. Give each student a blank index card and ask him or her to create a question that asks for an opinion or reflection on the course as a whole. The questions are then collected and put into a paper bag. Students randomly draw a question from the bag and write for a few moments. These could then be shared aloud as a whole group, shared aloud in small groups, or passed around for everyone to read. At the end of the activity, instructors can collect the cards and use them, if applicable, in future planning. In online classes, students are regularly asked to pose questions, but in the last session, these questions can be directed toward the whole class.

- Assign process letters or logs to accompany major projects or papers. Many courses require large papers, projects, or presentations that are due in the last sessions of a semester. Often these projects are content-based; however, students may have a lot to say about what they learned through the process of completing the project that does not make it into the project itself. Therefore, a number of instructors ask students to write a letter or keep a log that accompanies the work to reflect on the process. This piece may be worth a small amount of the total project grade, but it is valuable both to the student and the instructor.

- Use art to get students thinking. A fun activity to encourage reflection is to display images all over the room, such as photographs, prints, or ads. Students are then asked to select one or two images that best capture how they feel about the semester and what they learned from the course. Once students have found an image that represents their learning to them, they share those insights with the class as a whole or in small groups. Because students look to the art, rather than words, to help them express their feelings and ideas, this exercise can promote new ways of thinking about themselves and the course. This exercise can also be done with clay or random objects, by asking students to create a representation of their learning. This exercise encourages students to draw connections where they might not otherwise have seen them.

Create Opportunities for Celebration

Just as it is important to provide students with ways to reflect on their learning, it is also important to recognize students' desire for completion and celebration at the end of a semester. For many students, going to college demands both personal and familial sacrifice. Students may also give up time on the job in order to be in class. Because of these and other challenges, the completion of a course can be a powerfully rewarding and emotional experience. Instructors can encourage meaningful celebration in the following ways.

- Share food in the last class. It is a good idea to ask students whether this is something they want to do and to check with the college for any restrictions on bringing food into the facilities. Of course, this also depends on the size of the group. But many students and instructors do enjoy sharing food during the last class. It is a warm and friendly way to recognize the importance of that learning community.

- Present a fun activity after final presentations or exams. Because students often get anxious at these moments, this is a good opportunity to introduce a fun activity that also vents their nervousness. For example, students in a Shakespeare course might be asked to depict a character from *A Midsummer Night's Dream* while the class guesses the character's identity. In a business management class, students might be given a supply of different art materials and asked to develop, in small groups, the model of a successful leader or organization. Students then describe their creations and explain the thinking that went into the activity.

- In an online class, discussion questions or Web assignments can be designed to complement exams or projects that are due that week. For example, students in a literature course might be asked to tell a portion of a play or story from another character's perspective. Or they might develop the casting for the play or story using contemporary actors and describing how decisions were made. In a business course, students might be assigned a company to appraise online, deciding whether or not they would invest money or go to work there. They would then have to explain their reasoning. These kinds of activities are meaningful learning opportunities that also are fun.

- Play a game. Instructors could use a popular game-show format to review the material of the whole semester and emphasize how much students know as a result of taking the course. Some well-known games that are easy to modify for the classroom include Jeopardy (e.g., Computer Jeopardy), bingo (e.g., Psycho-Bingo), and Trivial Pursuit (e.g., Financial Pursuit). Students might be split into small groups and encouraged to work together in a collaborative manner. At the end of the game, all students could receive a small prize.

■ Read a poem, short story, or other words aloud to students. Many instructors like to find a short piece of writing that is connected to the course in some way and read it aloud at the last session. It may be inspirational or funny. It may also be something from the first class session that brings the course full circle. The most important element here is that the instructor is genuine, upbeat, and tactful in his or her remarks to students.

Anticipate Last-Minute Crises

Because community college students lead busy lives and are responsible for families, jobs, or other commitments, last-minute crises can occur (e.g., a family health emergency or loss of transportation or shelter). How an instructor handles this depends in part on the nature of the crisis and the individual student. Is the student calling to explain why he or she needs to reschedule the presentation? Or does the student want another week to complete the final project?

Of course, we want to be consistent in our own practices as instructors, which is why it is a good idea to address issues of attendance and late work in the very first class. However, there are times when an extenuating circumstance might mean an alteration in our expectations. This is a judgment call, but most of us find it helpful—when confronted with the student in crisis—to take a moment to consult with other instructors or the administration.

Develop Strategies for Evaluating Final Projects or Assignments

Of course, effective instructors assess and evaluate students throughout the semester in a balanced and varied manner. Even so, many instructors still assign projects or papers that are due at or near the end of the semester. Deciding how those projects or papers should be evaluated and what to provide for feedback can be a challenge. A few guidelines for evaluating students' last work are as follows.

■ Think about how the work will be evaluated before the assignment is given. Also, consider how much weight the assignment will be worth and convey this to students early on.

■ Use a rubric or other tool to help students understand how the work will be evaluated. Give the rubric to students at the time the work is assigned. In fact, rubrics work best when students are involved in their creation. (See the appendix for some sample rubrics.)

■ Provide students with a model or sample so they can visualize what a successful paper or project looks like before they complete it.

■ Align assignments and grading with course objectives so students are evaluated on their mastery of knowledge or skills.

■ Avoid grading students on a curve, which encourages competition between students and assumes that if everyone does well, there is something wrong with the content or the tool to measure learning. However, if all students perform poorly on an assignment or exam, consider rescaling the scores or revisiting the assessment tool.

- Evaluate work in a timely manner and return it to students promptly at the next class session. The longer it takes for students to get back assignments, the less effective the feedback is to them. In addition, students often resent having to submit work on a deadline when the instructor does not return work in a timely manner.

- Provide students with feedback that consists of more than a numeral or a letter grade. Narrative feedback, although time-consuming to write, is most conducive to learning. Even a few sentences summarizing the work as a whole can give students a sense of direction for the next assignment or course. In fact, instructors can focus some of their comments toward suggestions for improving performance in the future.

- Be clear about the problems in students' work but also be encouraging about what was accomplished. Many instructors limit the number of problems they address in an assignment, focusing on the three or four most important ones in an effort to give constructive, not overwhelming, feedback.

- Be as specific as possible. Avoid generalizations and do not judge the student's personal attributes. For example, rather than calling a student "industrious," describe his or her special effort to gather original source materials. Rather than calling a student irresponsible, note that she or he failed to complete several assignments on time. The general rule: Describe, do not label.

- Do not discuss a student's work with others in the class. Some instructors like to give the class a general sense of the work before returning it. For example, a business instructor might say to his class, "I was very excited to read these marketing plans and see how you incorporated our work of the last few weeks!" Or a math instructor might say to her students, "I noticed there were difficulties with one question, so let's go over it together to make sure we understand the concept." However, instructors do need to be careful in making statements about students' performance to the class; they risk damaging student morale and trust if the message is inherently negative. Under no circumstances should an instructor use a student's work in front of the class as an example of what not to do in an assignment.

- Decide ahead of time whether students who do poorly on an assignment will be allowed to resubmit it for a better grade, and discuss your policy at the beginning of the semester with students. Instructors might allow students to resubmit particular assignments and not others. In an effort to encourage students to improve their writing, instructors might allow them to revise any two assignments for a better grade. Other instructors may decide students cannot resubmit work but can take advantage of several extra credit options throughout the semester.

Developing Skills as an Instructor

Understanding Learning Styles

A student's learning style represents his or her preference for how to learn new information or skills. Some of us are natural observers who prefer a visual approach; some of us like to listen and reflect on what we hear. Still others of us might express our preference by saying, "I don't learn something until I actually experience it, try it out, and feel what it's like." Some people require complete silence before they can concentrate and study. Others can concentrate better with the TV or stereo on full blast. A room's lighting is critical to some people; a neat or cluttered environment makes a difference to others. Some learners rely on intuition and tend toward a more subjective approach. Others take a more objective stance and rely on logical thinking to solve problems. Some students are naturally interactive and benefit from the social aspect of a class. Others will display a more introverted, passive, and reflective approach. People obviously differ widely in how they learn, think, and behave. Therefore, it is worthwhile to consider two particular approaches to learning that have proven useful in higher education:

The Kolb Approach

David Kolb (Kolb, 1984; Kolb & Fry, 1975) developed a model that has been widely adapted and expanded on. When Kolb was a professor and freshman advisor at M.I.T., he was concerned that each year a certain percentage of the freshman students were struggling to keep up, discouraged with their performance, and generally unhappy with their programs. These students were as bright, qualified, and hard-working as any of the other students. Something, however, made them different.

Borrowing from the earlier work of John Dewey and Kurt Lewin, Kolb determined that people rely on four principal modes of learning: concrete experience, reflective observation, abstract conceptualization, and active experimentation. His findings suggest that to be effective, learners must involve themselves fully and openly in new experiences, reflect on what happened, determine what it means and how and where it applies, and experiment with their new ideas or take some action based on them. Although the action step completes the cycle of learning, the results can be fed into the next cycle and so on.

Kolb also discovered that people tend to have characteristic preferences for certain modes and combinations of modes (combinations indicate the actual learning styles) of learning that make up the cycle. In fact, the reason some of his advisees were struggling was that their particular learning style did not match the curriculum and instructional methods they encountered. These modes can be generally characterized in the following ways.

- Students with a strong orientation toward concrete experience will jump right into a new situation and experience it on an emotional/feeling level; they are likely to be more people-oriented and prefer exercises and hands-on experiences.

- Students who have a preference for a more passive, reflective approach to learning are comfortable watching and listening; they are more tentative, reflective, and impartial. They like lectures and presentations.

- Still other learners take an analytical and conceptual approach; they tend to be more oriented toward symbols. They may get frustrated by approaches that emphasize discovery—approaches such as simulation and role-playing.

- Finally, there are the students who are eager to apply what they are learning. Like those who prefer concrete experience, these students prefer an active approach to learning, but their actions are more structured and experimental in nature. These students thrive on projects, small-group discussions, and action-oriented homework assignments. They also tend to be extroverts and risk-takers.

The fact is that in any group of people, you can find different combinations of these preferences and modes. Because Kolb's model integrates two dimensions of cognitive growth and learning (active–passive and concrete–abstract) into a single framework, it has direct application to instructional design. Classroom activities can be arranged to mesh with the learning cycle and designed to provide opportunities for active learning and passive reflection, concrete experience and abstract idea formation.

To follow the learning cycle, an instructor has to plan a variety of activities and methods to ensure that the needs of different types of learners (auditory, visual, active, passive, etc.) will be met to some degree. The variety gives students opportunities to develop and grow by participating in activities that do not exactly match their preferred learning styles.

One approach is to begin a lesson with a specific activity (concrete experience) that gets students personally involved. According to Whitehead (cited in Mellert, 1998), at this stage in the education process students are "romanced" into learning. The next activity should stimulate students to reflect on the experience and figure out what it means (reflective observation). A brainstorming or similar exercise then allows students to draw some conclusions about the material and add some of their own ideas (abstract conceptualization). In the fourth part of the cycle, students apply the ideas to real-life situations (active experimentation) by interviewing someone, explaining the concepts, or tackling a case-study problem. To follow the learning cycle, an instructor has to plan a variety of activities and methods to ensure that the needs of different types of learners (auditory, visual, active, passive, etc.) will be met to some degree. The variety gives students opportunities to develop and grow by participating in activities that do not exactly match their preferred learning styles.

Gardner's Multiple Intelligences

Gardner's (1983) theory of multiple intelligences proposes that human beings have the capacity to process information in at least seven distinct ways and that each one of us has a particular set of talents and preferences in relation to these ways of knowing and learning. Because college classrooms in general tend to emphasize a few intelligences over others, it is especially worthwhile to consider the ways to enrich our teaching methods and reach students who otherwise might be left out of a "single-funneled approached to the mind" (Gardner, 1993, p. 33). The intelligences are described briefly as follows.

- Linguistic intelligence. Students strong in this area like to read, write, tell stories, join in discussions, and even listen to brief lectures.

- Logical-mathematical intelligence. These students are interested in figuring things out by questioning. They are interested in patterns, categories, and relationships, and they are good at math and problem solving.

- Body-kinesthetic. These students seem to always be in motion, using their bodies and hands to express ideas. They often excel at sports, dancing, and producing crafts.

- Spatial intelligence. These students think in images and pictures. They learn from drawing, designing, and looking at visuals. They are especially good at imagining, sensing changes, and reading charts and maps.

- Musical intelligence. Students who have strengths in this area are sensitive to rhythm, melody, and pitch. They often are found humming a tune, whistling, or singing.

- Interpersonal intelligence. These students are usually the joiners. They like group activities and are often good at leading, organizing, mediating, and understanding the feelings and ideas of others.

- Intrapersonal intelligence. These students perform well in independent activities. They know themselves and follow their instincts with confidence. They normally learn best when working individually in a self-paced project. They may be shy but are usually self-motivated.

Although the intelligences are listed separately, they rarely operate in isolation from one another. Students usually demonstrate a "melding" of several intelligences (Gardner, 1993, p. 17), so that an individual with kinesthetic intelligence may also express strong spatial and musical intelligence. It is also easier than one might imagine to integrate the seven intelligences into classroom activities. For instance, an American history instructor might create a lesson plan in which students, over the course of a few weeks, read and respond to letters from a certain time period, develop a strategy for and participate in a mock battle, analyze a patriotic song, and reflect on the commonalities between the lives of people in that time and our own. Another instructor might assign a research project and encourage students to demonstrate their knowledge to the class through one of the seven intelligences. One student might prefer to write and present a traditional research paper, whereas another student might prefer to create a working model. What is most important here is expanding the ways in which our classrooms are open to different styles of learning and different ways of knowing.

Building a Repertoire of Teaching Methods

Good instructors often draw from many sources and employ a variety of methods to build and facilitate a dynamic learning environment for students. Although methods do not in themselves make an instructor, the process of developing one's skills contributes to more than just technical expertise. Instructors who try new methods in the classroom are actively modeling for students the risks and rewards associated with learning. Situated in this way, we discover and rediscover ourselves as instructors.

Many of us may wonder, in our efforts to be effective, which instructional methods work best. Of course, there is so much to consider. Which teaching methods are we drawn to and why? Which methods do we avoid? Who are the students? What are the course objectives? How is the course scheduled? Even if we can answer all of these questions, most studies show that there is no one teaching method or single teaching style that is best for all students or for accomplishing all objectives. Nor is there a single method or style that works most effectively for all instructors. What does work is tapping into one's own passion or enthusiasm for a subject and using a wide variety of teaching methods. As one community college student commented at the end of a semester: "This class was great because we were always doing different things. We did small groups, videos, and in one class we acted out and resolved a conflict between a boss and her employee." To provide a variety of learning opportunities for students, we probably want to employ all of the methods described in this section.

Lecture

When we have information to share with our students, short bouts of lecturing can be an efficient way to do it. And most students, including adults, expect some lecture. A good lecture can do more than dispense information. It can demonstrate the logical reasoning and thinking patterns of the expert, and it can generate student enthusiasm for the subject.

Lecturing is not easy: A good lecture requires careful preparation, organization, and an attention-getting style of delivery. After all, this is the age of electronic media, and we must compete with it. In addition, lecturing may be more engaging for the lecturer than for the audience, so it is important to build in strategies for active involvement by students. All of these factors can make effective lecturing a challenge. Some tips for getting the most from this method are as follows.

Lecturing is not easy: A good lecture requires careful preparation, organization, and an attention-getting style of delivery. After all, this is the age of electronic media, and we must compete with it.

- Keep it short. During a lecture, students are in a relatively passive mode, so do not lecture more than 20 minutes without breaking for questions or discussion. Also, follow the lecture with an activity that requires active student participation.

- Organize lectures around problems that are relevant to students. According to McKeachie (1978), this technique is more effective than some other approaches and allows the instructor to weave in examples and evidence in such a way that the students begin to see the solution forming even before it is explained.

- Introduce the lecture with a summary (a type of advance organizer) and then wrap up the lecture with another summary that reviews not only the main points but also how the lecture accomplished its original purpose.

- Make the rules clear. Tell students whether they can interrupt or whether they should wait until the end to ask questions. Also, discuss the main objectives for the lecture, how long it will take, and whether students need to take their own notes.

- Some instructors provide students with an outline or abbreviated set of notes. This allows the students to listen without having to write at the same time.

- Punctuate lectures with brief question-and-answer periods or have students write one-sentence summaries of what has been covered to that point.

- Use visual aids to spruce up the presentation. In the past, overhead projectors often were used. Today, instructors may be more inclined toward Microsoft PowerPoint presentations of their lectures. However, it may be just as effective to use the blackboard, whiteboard, or newsprint. The essential element here is in using visual aids to complement the presentation or lecture.

- Some effective lecturers recommend that brief lecture periods are interspersed with small-group discussion or problem-solving sessions around one of the points presented. This keeps the class lively and energized, allowing students to process the lecture information actively.

Discussion

Discussion sessions, like effective lectures, require preparation and organization. They are more than informal chats with students. In fact, discussions can evolve into something beyond what an instructor might have planned. A good instructor needs to be aware of what is being discussed and how it is being discussed. Content and process learning are happening simultaneously. Who is talking to whom and for how long? How often? Which students are being analytical and which ones are not? Are some students always looking to the instructor for answers? A good discussion leader has to be a participant–observer, stepping back periodically to see what is going on. Still, discussion can be a powerful learning tool for both students and instructors, for several reasons:

A good discussion leader has to be a participant–observer, stepping back periodically to see what is going on.

- Discussions can develop critical thinking skills. Participants have to think about the questions asked, about what people say, and about how they want to respond. Discussion makes students process the content in a way that they then can articulate.

- According to McKeachie (1978), discussion exposes students to the logic and thinking patterns of others. Students are forced to evaluate the logic of and evidence for their own and others' positions. When students with different levels of ability interact with each other, growth and development are promoted.

- Students get to see and make connections between new ideas and what they already know. They can figure out ways to apply principles or solve problems using concepts already learned.

- Discussions can motivate students and provide a good setting for instructors to assess student progress.

However positive discussions can be for students, for the instructor they usually take some time and thought. Otherwise, discussions can get stalled or hijacked, ending up wasting everyone's time. Shor (1980) quoted a student in one of his own classes: "Teachers sometimes talk about things the students know nothing about and expect the students to comment on the discussion, but if they do not know anything about it they cannot participate" (p. 92). For some students, an academic discussion may feel like a game of chess they are forced to play without knowing the rules. However, instructors can help students enter the world of academic discourse through constructing learning environments where the most effective and engaging discussions can occur.

Students must feel absolutely secure that they can contribute without being ridiculed.

- Create an objective or goal. Ideally, each discussion should have its own objectives that are explained to students. Then, if the discussion gets too far off track, the instructor can bring it back by reminding students of the original purpose. For example, an instructor might say, "Remember our goal this morning is to define the problem in the case that was described, not to look for the solution." The objectives may provide enough structure to free students from unproductive ambiguity about what the instructor is doing.

- Establish ground rules for respectful communication. One of the most important considerations is to establish a climate of psychological safety in the group. Students must feel absolutely secure that they can contribute without being ridiculed. Instructors periodically should remind students that all questions are good ones and that all responses are worthy of consideration. This is why it is helpful to take even a few moments to consider students' comments before responding, especially when the comment may reveal an error. An instructor might ask a student who has made such a statement a few gentle questions, such as: "Why do you think that? How did you come to that conclusion?" It may be that the student's explanation reveals a unique and equally valid approach to the topic. For this reason, it is also a good idea to ask the same questions of students who appear to be correct in their assertions. When a student has made a comment that is flawed, it may be helpful to acknowledge the error as a necessary step in getting closer to the solution. This can be done in an upbeat and optimistic tone. For example, an instructor might say: "Mary, I'm glad you brought up that point because many of us get caught here in our thinking. It is helpful to consider why this is challenging…"

- Encourage students to participate without putting them on the spot. An instructor can help reluctant, shy, or insecure students by asking open-ended questions or soliciting their opinions rather than asking them for specific information or understanding. For example, an instructor might ask, "Bill, which of the author's arguments are most compelling for you?" or "Janet, how do you feel about this article?" Students are the best reporters of their own feelings, and even though the feelings may not match those of others, they cannot be challenged as being inaccurate.

- Vary discussion prompts or questions. Discussions can be started in a number of ways, for example, with a film clip, audiotape, or assignment. We can also prepare a brief demonstration, present a mini-lecture, design a role-playing exercise, or make a controversial statement. We might ask open-ended questions such as, "How might the reduction of the ozone layer in the atmosphere affect the lives of our children 20 years from now?" This is much more likely to stimulate a discussion than a question such as, "What is the ozone layer?" In fact, it is best to avoid questions that have one specific answer. With such questions, the discussion would be better served if the instructor gave the answer and then asked students to comment on the reasoning behind it. "Why do most experts believe the only way we can address the problem is through…?" Discussion can also be stimulated through presenting a case problem. A criminal justice instructor might begin by saying, "I want to tell you a little story about a man I will call Bill W…" and end with a question, "Who's at fault here for the tragedy of Bill W's life?" By first presenting a case study or problem to students in the form of a story, instructors engage and prepare them to participate in the discussion.

- Encourage student-to-student interaction. Arrange the seating so that people can make eye contact with each other. Paraphrase or comment on students' remarks to acknowledge, reinforce, and clarify their ideas. Gradually, get students to respond to each other similarly. In fact, instructors can facilitate this in the early stages by directing interaction: "Bill, Janine has outlined the major points in Skinner's theory. Can you think of ways that her knowledge of behaviorism could be applied in real-life situations?"

- Reflect on the group's process as well as the content of a discussion. From time to time during the discussion, summarize the progress the group is making, restate the current topic, and point out any impediments to the discussion. For example, an art instructor might say, "Well, we've done a good job of pointing out some of the factors that may have influenced the artist's creation of this sculpture, but let's move to how it was perceived by others after it was made. And I want to encourage you to stay in the middle of the 16th century. Try to discard your modern sensibilities, and imagine yourself there in that time and place. How do you see this sculpture, and why?"

- Give students a chance to be experts or consultants in the discussion. Ask infrequent contributors to comment when dealing in an area in which they have something to offer. This is a bit tricky because you want to encourage a sense of safety. But an instructor can acknowledge a student's expertise or interest with a few words. For example, an instructor might say, "Charles, you've done some initial research on this topic for your project. I wonder if you can share with us anything you've discovered that might relate to our discussion, even some of the reasons you were drawn to this topic in the first place." If some students are still reluctant to participate, give them room to be quiet observers. At a later time, instructors can talk to them individually about participating more. Also, instructors may need to break students into smaller groups for some of the discussion, because a large-group discussion can be intimidating to a number of people.

- Frame the discussion by offering students opportunities to do both independent and group thinking on the topic. Some students process their thoughts aloud and may not be aware of how much time they are taking up. Other students can get off-track and take the class with them in their meandering. In all these situations, it may be helpful for instructors to arrange for a pre-discussion activity. For instance, students can be asked to respond in writing first. These responses are not collected or graded by the instructor, but are simply a way for students to do some initial thinking about the topic. Students could also be given the opportunity to briefly share their thinking with a partner. In addition, instructors might give students the chance to check in with a partner throughout the discussion. These two-minute check-in sessions can energize students, keep the topic in focus, and meet the needs of both quieter and more active contributors.

- Allow silence. Develop a tolerance for silence and explain to students that difficult questions or problems sometimes require periods of thought before a good response can be made. If the discussion truly stalls or students seem to run out of steam, take a break. Sometimes students may be quiet because the topic or question is ambiguous or complex. In this case, it may be helpful to break down a large or complex question into smaller pieces and write them on the board. It may also be helpful to begin with a bit of free writing or split students into small groups to tackle different angles of the same question.

- Fully prepare for discussion by jotting down the questions you will use to start and direct the discussion. Be sure to plan both lower-order questions designed to elicit specific information and higher-order ones that get students to make connections and see parallels or contrasts. It also is important to think about the objective and the most salient points so that they can be restated for students at the end of the discussion. This can help instructors prepare for many of the different questions or comments students might have in response to the topic.

Online Discussion

Many classroom guidelines relate as well to online discussions. After all, discussion in the online classroom is essential to constructing the learning community. Unlike in the traditional classroom, students who do not actively participate are not given credit for being present. Many online instructors require students to contribute a minimum number of responses and questions. Of course, there is no reason to not participate. Many quieter students feel liberated in online discussion; they can take time to formulate their responses and questions, and they may feel less self-conscious about expressing their opinions.

However, there also are some unique challenges to designing effective and engaging discussion in this environment. Because this may encompass much of the students' interaction in a course, instructors want to create discussions that promote learning, reinforce academic skills, and sustain thoughtful and rich participation on behalf of students. Some of the guidelines for creating effective online discussion are as follows.

- Give choices. It is important to give students a variety of questions or topics to choose from in an online forum. Conversation might quickly grow redundant if 15 students are all responding to the same question. By constructing three or four dynamic questions, students can choose the ones that most interest them. This not only allows instructors to cover a wider range of topics, but it also strengthens the discussion as a whole because students are engaged and are offering their most meaningful responses.

- Ask open-ended and relevant questions. Discussion is not a way to test students on whether or not they have read the assignment. Questions that ask students to regurgitate information from their textbook will not promote a rich discussion in any classroom, online or not. Once a single student has answered the question, other students will be left with nothing to say. However, good questions can draw on readings or assignments in a meaningful way and allow students the opportunity to apply their learning and present alternate perspectives. For example, an anthropology instructor might follow an assignment on the mating rituals of a specific group by asking students to contrast these with American rituals around dating. The instructor might further ask students to speculate on American beliefs or values based on the rituals. A business instructor might follow a reading on marketing principles by asking students to shop for a product based solely on marketing campaigns and present their decision and rationale to others in the discussion.

- Think creatively and encourage active learning. In all our classes, active learning is key to getting students engaged. Adult learners tend to be more engaged when they are asked to solve problems and apply their learning to actual issues and situations. Instructors can do this through presenting case studies or problems. For example, a biology instructor might present a case on cloning and ask students to analyze several arguments for and against cloning only through a scientific perspective. Peirce (2001) described how analytical and critical thinking can be taught online through encouraging students to approach their assigned reading from varying perspectives or roles and then mediate between them. These different roles can be explored in asynchronous discussion. Instructors can also encourage active learning by using ancillary Web sites where students interact with specific material to formulate new ideas or a new context for their learning. These ideas can then be shared in discussion. For example, a writing instructor could direct students to view historical letters or diary entries and then create their own found poems.

- Be organized and simple in constructing the discussion. Although more and more students are familiar with the Internet, they may not be familiar with an online learning environment, especially one that involves a course management system. Therefore, it may take time for students to understand how to navigate material, link to other sites, and participate in asynchronous discussion. It is worthwhile for instructors to create a simple and organized format. After all, we want students to use their energies in thinking and responding to issues, not in decoding toolbars.

- Be consistent and maintain a customary schedule. Students expect classroom instructors to show up on time and hold class the full amount of time. Students also expect this of online instructors. Consistency is especially important to adult learners. At the beginning of the semester, instructors should explain to students how discussions will work, what the expectations for responding are, and when discussions will be closed or archived, if that is appropriate. It is important for instructors to then follow this schedule.

- Be present in discussion. Just as students need to be actively present in an online discussion by contributing responses and questions, instructors also need to be present. In a physical classroom discussion, instructors might nod or murmur in assent to show students that they are listening and engaged. In an online class, there is no way to do this except through a written response. Instructors must reply to students in order for students to know they are paying attention. Students need continual questioning, dialogue, and evaluative feedback for learning to be successful. This takes thought and energy on the part of the instructor. For example, an instructor might affirm a good point and ask a question to promote further thinking: "Good point, Heidi, about the weaknesses in this strategy, but what do you think are some of its strengths?" If the student presents information that is unclear, the instructor can address it diplomatically: "Chad, I think I understand what you're saying about _____, but can you explain a bit more about _____? I'm confused."

- Practice civility. There is no way for students to read an instructor's tone or body language, except through the written word. To make things a little more challenging, students themselves may have difficulty expressing their thoughts and feelings in writing. This can lead to a frustrating exchange for both student and instructor. Yet it is important to model a civil and respectful tone in all classroom discussions. If a student fires off an angry e-mail or discussion statement, it is best for instructors to take a bit of time to cool down before responding. Sometimes it is actually helpful to adopt a detached or dispassionate stance with the student. For example, an instructor might reply: "Lisa, you seem really frustrated by the reading assignment. What's most bothering you about the author's claim here? What points do you think he's most accurate about?" If the student's complaint is directed toward the instructor, he or she might let students know that the feedback is welcome but should be appropriate: "Jessie, I was disappointed to hear you found this assignment boring. Please let me know what might have made this more interesting and/or challenging for you. In the future, it might also be helpful for you to give me this feedback right away and by e-mail, rather than waiting until it is too late. I might have been able to offer you some suggestions for making this more interesting." In some cases, it may be appropriate for the instructor to respond to the student privately by e-mail rather than in a public discussion forum. If a student is disrespectful or disruptive in an online class, it may be necessary to take more drastic steps.

- Think ahead of time about how discussion will be evaluated and share that information with students at the beginning of the semester. Students need to know when, where, and how they will get feedback on their progress. Instructors may want to create a rubric or other criteria so that students can meet the expectations for discussion. In an online discussion, instructors want to think about how they will address and evaluate problems with grammar or mechanics, late submissions, and responses that do not relate to the topic or lack substance. As with any other assignment, the more detailed instructors can be in their expectations, the better students will be able to meet them.

Students need to know when, where, and how they will get feedback on their progress.

Small Groups

Breaking the class into small groups is a versatile and effective instructional tool. Commonly referred to as "buzz groups" because of the buzzing that can be heard in the room when students are hard at work, this technique is ideal for getting everybody actively involved in the class. Some students who are quiet in the large group will be enthusiastic small-group participants. It is easier for shy students to express their opinions in small groups because their contributions will be combined with other input and integrated into the group process. Many students also feel more comfortable having their ideas represented in this way because the collective "we" of a group can help alleviate some of the vulnerability inherent in the public setting of a classroom.

It is easier for shy students to express their opinions in small groups because their contributions will be combined with other input and integrated into the group process.

Small-group sessions are effective for brainstorming or analysis tasks, and they can be planned for appropriate points during a lesson. However, they can also be used to provide a context for the kind of connected learning in which students collaborate to solve a problem or develop a new interpretation of material. Some instructors even use them spontaneously when they sense the class slowing down and in need of a change. They are most effective, however, when instructors have prepared ahead of time a question, task assignment, or problem situation for students. Group membership can be randomly selected or carefully planned to provide a good mixture of styles and abilities. "Buzz groups" normally have three to six members and meet for about ten minutes. Each group picks a person to report back to the whole class. The instructor can circulate among the groups and even stop to share observations on occasion. Observing the small group action is another important tool for assessing how much learning is occurring and for determining which students are having problems. Small groups are also quite effective in the online environment and can promote more student-to-student interaction. Some tips for creating small group activities are as follows.

■ Assign groups a variety of tasks. For example, different groups can be assigned to research different aspects of a single topic or to take opposite sides of an issue.

■ Use small groups for role-playing or simulation games. Students are often able to take more risks in a group setting. This is also true in the online format. Students can work together to apply their knowledge and skills to case studies or problems and then explain to the rest of the class how they reached their conclusions.

■ Experiment with assignments that play on the strengths of individual students. Some members of a group can learn by observing how others handle an assigned task. Be sure to vary the types of tasks so that everyone gets a chance to show their strengths.

■ Use small-group discussions as follow-up to lectures and reading assignments. Put groups to work on projects and have them present their findings at the end of the period. If the class is small to begin with, instructors can break students into pairs. The small-group shift toward more active learning can help keep a class alive in the last minutes of a session. In the online format, the small-group shift can encourage more student-to-student interaction while enlivening discussions.

■ Ask small groups to participate in assessing aspects of the course or what is being learned. For example, each small group could review one of the learning objectives for the course, list the ways the objective has been addressed, and assess how well they have mastered it as a class. Small groups might also be used to assess the effectiveness of certain methods or texts. Instructors do not have to wait until the end of the semester to arrange these kinds of tasks. In fact, the more students are involved in creating the class, the better.

Role-Playing

If we make our subjects—our lessons—truly engaging, students tend to remember them. Duncombe and Heikkinen (1988) wrote about the memorable aspects of role-playing in an issue of *College Teaching*. For years, Duncombe, a political science professor, wore various hats in order to role-play different viewpoints in front of his classes. He found, to his amazement, that students did much better on exam questions about topics on which he had role-played than they did on most others.

Whereas Duncombe did this role-playing himself, many instructors get their students to do it. In typical, structured role-playing, instructors set a scene that partially replicates an actual situation related to the content of the course. Instructors ask students to assume parts and follow a loosely defined script or ad lib based on short written descriptions of their roles. For example, an education instructor might split students into pairs and ask them to act out a parent–teacher conference. Once they have had the opportunity to try out one role, the pairs switch and students assume the opposite role. At the end of the exercise, the instructor might ask students to reflect on the experience and develop some communication guidelines for public educators.

For years, Duncombe, a political science professor, wore various hats in order to role-play different viewpoints in front of his classes. He found, to his amazement, that students did much better on exam questions about topics on which he had role-played than they did on most others.

Role-playing can also be very effective in small groups. For example, an ethics instructor might assign each small group to act as a board of directors for a nonprofit agency. The instructor then presents the groups with challenging situations, such as a problem donor, negative press, or difficulty accounting for the use of certain funds. Small groups may even assume an extended role-play throughout the semester; an instructor teaching business and professional writing might assign small groups to create their own companies. Throughout the semester, the instructor relates to students both individually and in the context of their company roles. This kind of role-playing not only achieves a level of reality that engages students and makes learning fun, but when students assume professional roles in the classroom—even imaginatively—it also reinforces their suitability for such roles in real-life. This is especially important for students who may not have access to other models in their fields. The following are some tips for using role-playing in the classroom.

■ As with other methods, be sure to outline the purposes of the role-playing exercise.

■ Role-plays are good for practicing skills, applying concepts, and developing problem-solving abilities.

■ Do not be afraid to experiment. Even the simplest role-play can be fun and informative, and the class may gain from asking why certain roles were difficult to play.

■ Give specific instructions to any non-player observers. Ask them to report their observations after the role-play.

■ "I think we have reached a good stopping point" is an appropriate way for instructors to end the session. Depending on the type of role-playing, 10 to 20 minutes may be plenty long enough.

■ Paradoxical intention is a useful technique. In this approach, instructors ask the players to do it the wrong way. For example, in a business course on supervision, an instructor might ask a player to exhibit poor listening skills in a conflict management scene. After a time, the player could be asked to switch styles and exhibit strong listening skills.

- Role reversal is a related technique where instructors ask participants to change roles to an opposite type of character and continue with the scene. When students act out and experience differing points of view, they broaden perspectives and develop a more objective stance on issues.

- Debriefing is a critical aspect of role-playing. Players should give a quick summary of how they felt and what they learned playing their roles. Observers can report their impressions. Instructors can ask students to integrate the results of the role-play with the material learned in class or from readings.

Other experiential methods include simulations, field trips, laboratory work, interviewing, and survey research. These hands-on approaches to learning can enhance the teaching and learning of a new concept. They match the learning styles of many students, they energize and add variety to the instructional program, and they promote active student involvement in the learning process. Many instructors have found that using one of these methods to introduce a new concept provides a shared experience that can make subsequent discussions or other activities more relevant and meaningful.

Case Studies

Using case studies or problems in the classroom can help engage learners, introduce multiple perspectives, promote critical thinking, connect theory to practice, and enhance problem-solving and cooperative learning skills. Case studies often are used in educating students in the areas of law and business, but students in almost any discipline can benefit from this active-learning technique. Case studies are, at their most basic, stories that relate in some way to the content of our courses. As stories, they are naturally engaging and provide a rich context for the more abstract theories and principles than students are regularly required to learn.

Herreid (1997), writing in the *Journal of College Science Teaching*, drew on research done at Harvard University and the Kennedy School of Government to present guidelines for finding or creating a good case-study problem. Those guidelines have been adapted to present the following criteria for an effective case problem:

- It takes the form of a story. A good case study usually has a beginning, middle, and end, even when briefly stated. By employing the elements of a good story, the case quickly hooks the listener.

- It focuses on an issue or drama. Just like a good story, the case problem presents a situation that has some element of suspense. In addition, a good case will promote a sense of empathy. Quotations may be used so that students can better relate to the characters in the case.

- It is current and relevant. In order for case studies to be most engaging, they must have a problem or issue that contemporary students find compelling. This also makes the case something students will consider worthwhile to study.

- It is related to the course material. There may be a good case problem in business management, but unless it is related in some way to his or her course objectives, a psychology instructor may not want to use it with students. Before using any case study, it is important for instructors to ask themselves what purpose it serves. How is it related to the course? What will students gain from the activity? Certainly, instructors can ask students to reflect on the case and its connection to the course, but instructors should be thinking about these same questions before they present a case to the class.

- It is complex, encouraging different perspectives. Often, a good case is controversial and can provoke debate. It has a sense of urgency about it, compelling students to think long and hard about the issues contained within the problem. This also forces students to come to a decision or make a choice in their thinking.

- It is general enough. If a case is too unique or unusual, students will not be able to apply their learning to it. It will not seem real or plausible enough to compel serious thought either to defining the problem or solving it.

- It presents a manageable scope. A good case problem or study must have enough detail to hold students' attention but not so much detail to detract students from their task with it. If the case is too long, it may become boring or so complex as to be frustrating for students.

Once instructors have cases that meet these guidelines, they can use them in various ways to promote active learning. They might, for example, follow a mini-lecture with a case problem. They might split students into small groups to work with a case, assigning each group a different aspect of the problem. They might even assign students specific roles or perspectives from which to explore the case. It is a good idea for instructors to begin the case study activity by encouraging students to raise issues and ask questions that have nothing to do with their own beliefs or value systems. In fact, instructors might ask students to explore all perspectives, even ones with which they disagree.

In any case, there are many options for instructors in deciding what they want students to address. Instructors may ask students to focus their discussion not on solving a problem but on defining the problem. This is more challenging than most students realize and is a good way to illustrate how we differ in our perceptions.

Audiovisual Instruction

Films, videos, DVDs, slides and other audiovisual materials are available on many subjects. However, instructors want to think carefully about using them to promote active and engaged learning. Here are some general considerations for working with these materials in the classroom.

- Instructors should become familiar with any equipment before they use it. Instructors can avoid embarrassing glitches by testing the equipment and their skill at using it ahead of time. Also they should review the materials before class, even to the extent of testing the material with the equipment to be used in class.

- Instructors should provide students with plenty of background information. The objectives for using the material should be clear, and the presentation can be followed with more discussion so that students can see the connection between the presentation, course readings, and other learning activities.

- Whenever instructors use video or other audiovisual material in the classroom, it is important to keep active learning opportunities in mind. Some instructors show an excerpt of a video and ask students to identify specific aspects. For instance, a history instructor might present a film excerpt and ask students to find as many anachronisms as possible. A communications instructor might present the beginning of an interaction between characters in a television comedy or drama. Students could then be asked, in small groups, to brainstorm the different ways the interaction might conclude. Used alone, video can be a very passive medium, but combined with activities, it can be enriching for students.

■ Above all, instructors should avoid overuse of these materials, aiming instead for presentations that add to or complement the lesson and serve a specific purpose.

Combining Methods

Because our students reflect diversity, so must our teaching methods. Even if it appears that all students in a class are absorbing information from the traditional lecture, it is important to use other methods, because each method encourages or builds different skills. Students need exposure to and practice with these methods. By developing our repertoire of methods, we also demonstrate our flexibility in teaching and our commitment to learning. The following ideas can be used to enhance and supplement the strategies mentioned so far.

■ Individualize activities, projects, and papers when necessary. Sometimes this is the only way to ensure that a certain student will learn a particular concept or skill. Students can report on research findings, describe the work of their small group, or demonstrate a skill. In other words, think about your essential goals for any assignment or lesson, and then consider alternate ways those goals can be achieved.

■ Combine methods whenever possible. Combine lectures with small-group discussions and discussion periods with an experiential exercise. Flip-flop the groups; get half the class to work on a writing assignment while the other half does research or a case scenario exercise.

Some instructors begin each class with an icebreaker or quick brainstorming session to help students make the transition from home or work to school. Such exercises reinforce the idea that students not only have something valuable to contribute in each class, they have a responsibility to do so.

■ Use brainstorming techniques to generate ideas and draw on students' creativity. Start off with a question like: "How many ways can you think of to use this skill in an office environment?" Remind students that there are no dumb or impossible ideas in brainstorming and that no criticisms are allowed. Break into small groups and have each group take the list, rank the ideas, and identify or expand on the most plausible or creative suggestions. Some instructors begin each class with an icebreaker or quick brainstorming session to help students make the transition from home or work to school. Such exercises reinforce the idea that students not only have something valuable to contribute in each class, they have a responsibility to do so.

■ Avoid meltdown. Within a single class session, group energy can sag. Students can sit only for so long without needing to stretch, drink, or otherwise move around. Take breaks accordingly. Mixing up your methods allows students to make mental shifts or breaks, but it also is important to follow stretches of sustained concentration with something lighter.

■ The last minutes of class can also get dull, even if we are strategic in planning breaks. Instructors may feel the sag themselves. Plan ahead and jazz up that period: recap, highlight, or plan an engaging activity, something to energize the whole class.

■ At about the seventh or eighth week of a 15-week semester, enthusiasm for the whole enterprise may wane. This is a good time to do a role-play, get a film, play a game, take a field trip, or invite a guest speaker. Think about this week in particular when creating the semester's lesson plan. Create opportunities for engagement and fun.

Developing Students' Writing, Thinking, and Speaking Skills

It is only when we move away from the notion that all writing should lead to formal products, such as the traditional research paper, that we appreciate the central role of writing as a means of learning.

During the semester, much of what we teach students is connected to the learning objectives associated with our specific courses; after all, we use these objectives or goals to plan our assignments, our lessons, and our exams. Still, whatever we teach, we also need to invest in developing students' overall academic skills, especially those in writing, critical thinking, and speaking. This does not mean that a computer instructor is responsible for teaching students how to write an essay, or that a psychology instructor is responsible for teaching students how to think quantitatively. It does, however, mean that students need opportunities to develop and practice their academic skills in courses across the curriculum. As we develop our repertoire of teaching and evaluation methods, it is worthwhile to consider how our activities and assignments contribute to building students' skills. By choosing methods that develop students' writing, thinking, and speaking, we send a clear message to them that these skills are essential to learning our course content. Students who are held accountable in courses across the curriculum are better able to integrate their learning as a whole.

The movement toward integrating writing across the curriculum (WAC) has been active in colleges for the last several decades. According to Stout and Magnotto (1988), community colleges and WAC programs share a similar belief that just as almost all people can learn—with supportive and effective instruction—so, too, can they write. In addition, "WAC programs can serve the technical and vocational curricula integral to community colleges by emphasizing writing to learn and writing that is likely to help graduates become promotable employees" (Stout & Magnotto, 1988, p. 24). It is only when we move away from the notion that all writing should lead to formal products, such as the traditional research paper, that we appreciate the central role of writing as a means of learning. In doing so, we focus on the issues that unify all instructors, "such as what constitutes literacy and what we mean by informed teaching in general" (Soven, 1988, p. 20).

Alternative Writing Assignments

No matter what we teach, we want students to write effectively. We also want students to undertake research—to locate relevant and credible sources, to evaluate them, to use them effectively to support their argument, and to give appropriate credit for them. As you might imagine, this presents a stiff challenge for new students. Writing a college-level paper is itself a complex task, but when we add research to the mix—as in the traditional research paper assignment—we increase the difficulty exponentially.

Knowing how to write a college-level research paper is a necessary and valuable skill for students, one that is addressed in detail in most freshman composition courses. We also know that it is essential for students to have the opportunity to write, speak, and think critically in every class. And yet, this does not necessarily mean that we should assign traditional research papers in all our courses. In fact, other kinds of writing and research assignments may be more effective in helping students to develop and refine their skills. Consider the following alternatives to the traditional research paper.

- Multiple short papers. Consider assigning several short papers rather than a large paper. Because the scope of a large paper can seem overwhelming to a student, she or he may choose a broad topic, gather too much information, and put off the actual writing process. By assigning shorter, more focused papers, we can lessen a student's panic and target his or her thinking on critical aspects of the topic. For example, in a social science course, we might ask students to compare two films (or photographs) in one aspect only—the way gender, class, or race is depicted. By giving students some choice in their approach but narrowing the possibilities, we are directing students' energy into forming ideas and supporting them—critical areas for beginning college students.

■ Annotated bibliography. Consider dropping a paper altogether and substituting an annotated bibliography and teaching presentation. Annotated bibliographies are a great way to reinforce the skills associated with gathering and evaluating sources. By asking students to focus their research on a specific topic, instructors can emphasize the importance of finding academically credible sources in their given fields. In addition, this kind of assignment requires students to evaluate their sources for relevance and usefulness. Students then present a lesson to their classmates, using their new knowledge to teach others about an aspect of the topic.

■ Case scenarios or problem-solving papers. Consider creating a set of course-related scenarios or problems to which students can apply their knowledge of a topic. For example, education or business students could be asked to create a teaching curriculum or workplace solution to a set of problems. Students in a mythology course might be asked to write a proposal for a nature park based on Celtic culture and beliefs or create a magazine article based on the discovery of a religious artifact. This kind of assignment not only appeals to many students, it also encourages them to think both critically and creatively about their topics. Rather than regurgitating material from their sources, students are forced to consider how they might use their research to address their challenge or problem. This assignment also reinforces the concept of audience. Beginning college students often have difficulty with perceiving the audience for their papers as anyone other than their instructors, resulting in problems with tone and purpose. Finally, this kind of assignment is also interesting for instructors to both create and evaluate.

■ Controlled sources. Consider developing a set of resources related to a topic and asking students to write papers using those sources to support their theses. For instance, instructors might develop a set of resources on topics such as acid rain, homelessness, Internet advertising, the Korean War, or adoption laws. The possibilities are endless. In fact, instructors might create several sets of resources, each on a different topic related to their course. Each student, in turn, could be asked to contribute one or two resources of her or his own or as part of a group. In this way, instructors and students could develop and discuss the criteria for including a source in the set. This kind of assignment is especially beneficial to students because it emphasizes the development and support of ideas. It builds students' skills in reading and analysis and directs their energy toward incorporating sources rather than finding them. As a result, students spend more time understanding the topic through reading and writing and less time collecting general or misguided information. In addition, instructors have the opportunity to present the types of sources that are most appropriate for college-level research in their fields. When students are expected to find their own sources for a paper, they will have a better idea of what that means.

The reason these assignments are offered as an alternative to the traditional research paper is not because there is anything wrong with expecting students to write one. In fact, annotated bibliographies, controlled sources, and case scenarios reinforce the very skills required to complete a college-level research paper. But in these alternative assignments, the skills are broken down and addressed separately, allowing students to direct their energies toward the mastery of one or two skills in the complex series that is essential to effective research and writing. This is similar to the way a coach might work with an athlete to help refine his or her physical skills. Whether we use an alternative research assignment or a traditional one, there are some simple things we can do to help students and get better results. For example, we can spend more time thinking about what we want from students and designing assignments that reflect this.

Designing Effective Assignments

Designing effective writing assignments is a lot like designing any good assignment. Experience tells us that the more detailed we are about our expectations, the better it is for students. This is because, in part, our expectations vary widely when it comes to student writing. Some instructors advise students not to write in the first person, whereas others admonish students against regurgitating what experts think about their topic. Some instructors require a thesis in their papers; others dismiss the thesis and encourage students to take a more informative stance. Because students come to our classes with diverse backgrounds and varied experience with writing, it is especially important to set clear guidelines. The following are some tips for constructing effective writing assignments.

- Less is more when it comes to page requirements. Large papers often contribute to a student's worst inclination: unfocused, padded, generalized writing. When we assign one large paper in our courses, we leave little opportunity for students to make progress in their writing. It is better to assign a number of small papers.

- Build in due dates for topic selection and drafts. Instructors are more likely to catch problems early on if they have established deadlines for parts of a large or complex assignment. Ask students to submit a proposal for a final project five or six weeks before it is due. Follow this up with at least one draft. These will not take a lot of time to correct, but they will help instructors catch those students who are totally off-track. Multiple deadlines also provide a strong deterrent to plagiarism and will help students better manage their time.

- Give students options in their choice of topics or assignments. It is important for students to feel connected to their writing. The more interested they are in the assignment, the better the results. It also is good to give students options in the essay sections of their exams; for example, an instructor might ask students to choose one of four essay questions to address. The important point here is to create opportunities for investment. Both Nodding (1995) and Rodgers (1969) have endorsed the practice of allowing students choice in learning activities and assignments.

- Detail exactly what is expected. The more precise instructors are in their guidelines, the better results they will get from students. When instructors initially conceive of an assignment, they should spend time visualizing what they want to receive from students. Being as concrete as possible, they should describe their assumptions and expectations in writing. They can then give these out as guidelines for the assignment and go over them verbally. Instructors who are interested in creating student-centered classrooms may even use their initial goals for an assignment as a way to negotiate concrete details with the class.

- Allow students to brainstorm on topics or share their writing in class. If possible, allow students to read through some of their ideas and brainstorm in small groups. This will help them to think about the audience for their writing and emphasize the need for clarity. When students share ideas and writing with each other, they encounter the notion of an audience broader than just their instructor. Also, students who have difficulty with their own writing may gain insight from examining others' writing. The process for sharing can be very simple for all; ask small groups to develop a list of questions related to each student's paper. Small groups might also act as consultants

Instructors are more likely to catch problems early on if they have established deadlines for parts of a large or complex assignment. Ask students to submit a proposal for a final project five or six weeks before it is due.

to the student writer, serving as a sounding board for the process, not the product. Of course, any activity requires some thoughtful planning and implementation, but instructors across the curriculum can reinforce the importance of writing skills with a little effort in this area.

■ Give model papers as examples. Using student models of writing in our classes can be very effective. All writers appreciate clear expectations, and nothing is clearer than a visual model. However, more important than the models themselves is how we use them. We should never hand out copies of a student's paper in order to denigrate it. In fact, many instructors avoid using essays from the current semester and mask the identity of the previous semester's authors, having obtained their permission. Model papers do not necessarily have to serve as exemplars either. One of the reasons students' papers work well as models is that students can relate to them. Instructors might disburse several different papers related to a specific assignment and ask students in small groups to rank them or evaluate them. This exercise could lead to the development of a class rubric or help students to simply visualize the priorities associated with the particular assignment.

■ Do not assume anything. Many of us have learned this the hard way. Even if a student has written a position paper before, it does not mean his or her idea of a position paper is the same as ours. When assigning any written work, be prepared to tell students what it is and how it should be done. Instructors vary widely in their expectations for college writing, so it is a good idea for instructors to test out their assignments on someone who is unfamiliar with the course. See how they might interpret the guidelines.

■ Show students how their work will be evaluated. Do not wait until students turn in their papers to decide how they will be evaluated. If instructors create a rubric or other evaluation tool, it should be shared with students early on. Students may even participate in creating the evaluation criteria for an assignment. Any evaluation tool is helpful in clarifying our expectations and makes students more likely to submit the kind of work we are seeking.

■ Build in opportunities for reflection. Whatever the assignment, give students the chance to reflect on the writing they complete. Some instructors assign students to complete a process letter in which they reflect on why they chose the topic and what they learned from the assignment. Instructors might also hand out a questionnaire after assignments, asking students to report anonymously on particular aspects of the work. Other instructors design a reflective piece right into the writing assignment itself, asking students to respond to a topic outside their experience and knowledge. Again, when we ask students what they think and how they feel about their work, we create opportunities for relevance and engagement.

Guidelines for Evaluating Writing

For many instructors, evaluating students' writing is even more challenging than assigning it. However, by keeping the following simple ideas in mind, you can respond effectively to student papers and feel comfortable doing it.

■ Avoid using a red pen. Many students have a negative memory associated with red ink and writing. None of us wants to trigger a student's past feelings of anxiety or failure.

■ Address the writer of the paper from the perspective of a reader, not the ultimate authority. Ask questions and respond to the ideas as well as the mechanics. This not only takes the pressure off instructors around correcting troublesome writing, but it also helps students to better absorb the feedback provided by instructors. For example, an instructor might write one of the following: "I don't fully understand the point you're making here. I think you're saying _____, but an example might have helped me." "This opinion seems out of place or unsupported. Perhaps you needed to rethink its purpose for being in your paper." "This is a large topic, and you've done a nice job summarizing its general qualities, but I need more focus and depth. Perhaps you could have selected one of your ideas here to explore further. The third and fourth paragraphs seem to have a lot of energy and liveliness in their writing. What about those?" "I feel like you got off-track with this part. I think it's an interesting aspect to consider, but it really distracted me from your main point." Of course, how we frame our comments has a lot to do with the stage of a student's paper. If it is a first or second draft, our comments can be much more open and suggestive toward a future revision. However, if we are examining a student's final draft, it may seem fruitless to point out, "You seem to be reversing your opinion here; you need to take a stand on this position, even if it's one shaped from both sides of the issue." After all, the paper is complete; yet students can benefit immensely from open and suggestive feedback, if not with the paper in hand, certainly with future papers or future thinking around the topic.

■ Give opportunities for revision. If there are deadlines for a paper's first and final draft, students will receive the message that papers are revised and well written for every class, not just composition. Instructors can also have a rewrite grade, which is assigned whenever students turn in a paper that is unacceptable; the grade means students must re-submit the paper for any credit at all. Some instructors also allow students to turn in a paper as many times as they want for a better grade as long as they initially turn it in on time. An instructor's magnanimous style can pay off in reduced anxiety and improved papers.

■ Balance comments between the positive and negative. As is to be expected, students are sensitive about their writing. When instructors take the time to address both the strengths and the weaknesses of a paper, students are more likely to see the feedback as reasonable. For instance, an instructor might write: "One thing that seems to be working really well is your tone in the essay, which captures the urgency of the issue but also seems open and fair. However, I'm concerned about the organization, because some of your most persuasive points get bunched together and, thus, lost."

■ Limit negative comments to the three or four most troubling areas. Anything more than three or four criticisms will be too much to absorb and can actually sabotage a student's writing. It is much more effective to read a student's paper from start to finish, and then determine what the major issues are. That way, instructors can, in their comments, impart a sense of scope.

■ Think about how your evaluation tool reinforces your values around writing. Some instructors provide students with two or three grades for every paper: ideas, structure, and mechanics. They hope students will clearly see the impact of problems, and may be more motivated to get help. Other instructors feel strongly that any separation between writing and content sends the wrong message to students. For these instructors, writing is the content, because any division of ideas from how they are

Balance comments between the positive and negative. As is to be expected, students are sensitive about their writing. When instructors take the time to address both the strengths and the weaknesses of a paper, students are more likely to see the feedback as reasonable.

expressed is artificial. Still other instructors use a rubric that breaks down the components of the assignment and gives a concrete description of each. Rubrics work well when given at the time of the assignment; however, they may work best when students have a voice in their creation.

■ If the paper needs help, be sure to let students know where they can get assistance. Most community colleges have a strong network of academic support for students. Many have writing centers where students can meet one-on-one with specially trained instructors or tutors. There are also workshops pertaining to grammar and research offered at many colleges. Also, there is a rising number of online writing labs available for students. These may be sponsored by the college itself or by outside providers. The important thing is to find out what resources are available for students and direct them accordingly. When instructors assign writing early and often in their courses, they have a good handle on who needs additional support.

Methods for Preventing Plagiarism

More and more, we hear about incidences of plagiarism in our high schools and colleges and even among our most respected writers. Some students feel a sense of entitlement to information on the Internet, where it seems that almost everything is free for the taking. In fact, whole papers can be downloaded for little or no cost. Sometimes these services for papers are even advertised on the legitimate Web sites students use for research. Each college will define plagiarism in its own way; however, in general, plagiarism is presenting another person's language, ideas, or thoughts as one's own work.

Even when students do not set out to plagiarize, they may do so inadvertently. Many students do not fully understand what plagiarism is and how to avoid it. They may cut and paste excerpts from Internet sources into their papers and then forget to provide the appropriate citation and quotation marks. They may include a source citation at the end of their paper but neglect to reference it anywhere in the body of the paper. They may fail to properly paraphrase from a source. In fact, depending on a student's experience in this area, some incidences of plagiarism may be a result of mixed messages students have received. For example, students are routinely told to defer to expert opinions on a topic, and yet when students use a lot of quoted or paraphrased material, they are charged with creating choppy or disjointed writing. As a result, they may be told to distinguish between information that is common knowledge—and need not be cited—and information that is expert opinion. However, skills of this kind are sophisticated and still developing for many undergraduates.

We know it is important to assign writing in our courses—all our courses—to build students' skills. Yet when we assign writing, we need to be aware of plagiarism and the methods for deterring, detecting, and dealing with it. Of course, our first step in preventing plagiarism is to create effective assignments. Next steps might include the following.

■ Provide clear, concise instructions for all assignments. If an assignment is detailed enough, students will be less likely to use a plagiarized paper to meet the guidelines. Understand where students are likely to have difficulty with an assignment, and offer special instructions for those areas.

■ Be creative in developing assignments; think about offering students the opportunity to apply their learning in diverse ways. For example, students in a management course might write a traditional research paper, write an analysis of an historical leader or manager, or write a case study of a local business with management problems.

- Speak to the entire class early in the semester about plagiarism. When assigning a research paper or other work, begin by reading aloud the college's policy on academic honesty. Some instructors ask students to sign a statement that they have abided by this policy when they turn in work to be graded. This further reinforces, psychologically, the importance of academic honesty.

- Teach students what plagiarism is and what the penalties are for committing it. Many students do not intentionally plagiarize; however, failure to understand what plagiarism is does not protect students from the consequences of engaging in it. Students found to be dishonest in academic work may be subject to disciplinary action, which can include suspension or dismissal. Therefore, it is useful for instructors to spend at least a short time in class going over the proper method for citing sources in the body of a paper, because this is often unclear to students. Also, it is helpful when instructors demystify the idea of plagiarism by using metaphors and other examples that students can understand.

- Create meaningful assignments for students, ones that are relevant and allow students to make choices in their topics. Students are less likely to plagiarize when an assignment is interesting and relevant to them.

- Break up a large, complex assignment into stages, and assign different due dates for each stage. Use other students in the classroom to act as writing peers and devote small chunks of classroom time for students to give feedback to each other on their most important assignments.

- Require students to submit copies of their resources or reference notes and their writing drafts with their final papers. We can emphasize the idea that the research project is a process and that we are interested in the whole endeavor, not just the finished product.

- Use college resources as needed, including library services, writing centers, tutors, online presentations, and support systems.

Detecting and Addressing Plagiarism

Of course, even if we create meaningful and well-constructed assignments, we may still receive papers that are plagiarized in part or in whole. Although instructors should never assume a work has been plagiarized without thoroughly investigating, there are some warning signs that might indicate a possible problem:

- The bibliography contains sources that are old or obscure or sources with dates you recognize as wrong.

- The paper or written product is mismatched in appearance, suggesting that pieces may have been cut and pasted into the document from other sources.

- There is a marked difference in quality, thinking, or writing from previous work. (This also illustrates the benefit of assigning writing throughout the semester, so that instructors become familiar with a student's style.) Do not assume that a plagiarized piece will be better written than a student's own essay.

- The writing includes curious or distinctive use of words or phrases.

- The work does not fit the guidelines of the assignment (e.g., the student leaves out parts of the assignment, like an annotated bibliography or an outline.)

- The student has changed topics more than once or in a late manner, but the paper reflects extensive research.

If you suspect a paper has been plagiarized, in part or in whole, it is important to thoroughly investigate the matter before speaking to the student. Some tips for dealing with a case of suspected plagiarism are as follows.

- Adequately prepare for the meeting with the student.

- Review the college's policy on academic honesty or plagiarism.

- Recognize that it is difficult to confront a student.

- Arrange to talk to the student about the issue in a private setting, and really try to listen to what the student has to say. Do not jump to conclusions.

- Be respectful of the student even when disagreeing with the student's actions or excuses.

- Inquire about the issue, drawing the student out; ask questions about how the work was created or what process was used. (For example, an instructor might say: "This work appears to be a departure from earlier work you have submitted. Can you tell me what changed for you?")

- Ask to see the student's sources for a paper (or other important material for an assignment).

- Bring guidelines of the assignment, the evaluation rubric or other tool, and the college's policy to the meeting.

- Conduct an Internet search or other investigation before the meeting. It is important to have support for a claim of plagiarism. Although there are various college and Internet services to assist instructors, the easiest way to conduct an Internet search is to find distinctive phrases from the paper and, using a search engine with key-word capacity, run a check.

- If you encounter a case of unintentional plagiarism, be sure to bring information on the correct method for citing sources and give concrete examples to identify the problem. (Even if the college's policy does not distinguish between intentional and unintentional plagiarism, it can be helpful to distinguish between them when talking to the student.)

Probably no instructor looks forward to having a conversation about suspected plagiarism with a student. However, if we are to combat academic dishonesty and teach students how to negotiate between others' ideas and their own, we must address incidents as they occur in our classes. It is through preventing, detecting, and dealing with plagiarism that we teach students about the power and responsibility of using language to express ideas.

Integrating Writing, Thinking, and Speaking in the Classroom

Although assignments do some of the work of developing students' skills, they cannot do it all. In fact, classroom activities may be as effective—or more effective—than assignments because students can work with others, get immediate feedback from instructors and peers, and practice their skills without the pressure of being graded. Many of the exercises we do in the classroom promote writing, thinking, and speaking. The following are some particularly useful activities.

- Reaction writing. This exercise can be done in any course and is a great warm-up for discussion. It also does double-duty for most instructors as it can address students' homework. Instructors begin the class session by writing three or more questions on the board related to the assigned reading. Students then choose one question to respond to and write for a period of 10 or 15 minutes. Groups are created on the basis of the questions students chose. Each group discusses the original question and any others that might be posed by the instructor who circulates among the groups. After a short discussion period, one or more students from each group present a summary to the whole class. Writing in this way builds self-esteem during discussions. Students can be more fully open to others' ideas because they have had the opportunity to mentally process their own ideas through writing. Also, because the writing is neither collected nor graded by instructors, students learn to associate writing with thinking on paper.

- Critical-thinking problems. Many students become actively engaged when dealing with a problem, a riddle, or a challenge of some type. Instructors can use relevant problems to pique interest, develop critical-thinking skills, and make connections between theory and practice. Some instructors introduce a problem at the beginning of the class session, giving students some time in small groups to work through it. If the groups do not solve the problem, the instructor moves on in the lesson, coming back to the problem at the end of the class. By introducing the problem early on, the instructor may help students stay engaged throughout the class. There is wide variety in the type of problems that can be used by instructors. A communication or writing instructor might present a riddle to emphasize the effect of ambiguity and assumptions in language. A math instructor might present a strategic problem from real life in order to illustrate the importance of logical and quantitative thinking. A computer instructor might present a complaint posed by a customer to his or her computer support services, giving students the opportunity to diagnose what the problem is and how to address it.

- Small-group decision making. Any work in a small group reinforces students' thinking and speaking skills. However, instructors can take this even further by assigning students to make decisions and develop a rationale that is presented to the rest of the class. In many ways, this kind of exercise mimics the skills students need to complete a research project. For example, political science students might be given the task of developing the five most important qualities in an effective gubernatorial candidate. Students begin by developing their own lists of qualities and then meet in small groups to achieve consensus. At this point, they then create a rationale that can be persuasively presented to the whole class. Just as in developing a research paper, students brainstorm their own ideas, research what others (their group members) think, develop a thesis (the qualities they choose), and support it with evidence (their rationale).

- Student-generated questions. Too often in our classes it is the instructor who has the most practice in developing thoughtful and pertinent questions. Yet being able to pose effective questions or develop problems is a challenging skill that promotes critical thinking. In online classes, instructors regularly ask students to submit questions for discussion and give feedback on how to do this. We need to implement more of this in our classrooms. Students can work in small groups to develop questions for exams or discussion. Instructors can also distribute blank index cards, asking students to write down a question that relates in some way to the current course lesson and solicits an interpretation or opinion (rather than a yes/no answer). Instructors collect these questions, place them in a paper bag and redistribute them to the class. Students then respond to the questions they receive and the class shares aloud both questions and responses.

- Peer teaching. Although it takes time to use peer-teaching techniques in the classroom, instructors can be relatively sure that students learn and retain the material they teach others. Students also develop critical thinking and speaking skills. Some instructors assign small groups to present a mini-lesson to the class. Other instructors may assign individual students to take responsibility for one assigned reading per semester. Students then provide the class with a summary, one or two discussion questions, and supplementary material that is connected to the reading. This might be a newspaper article, a piece of music or art, or an artifact.

Integrating Service Learning in Courses

Service learning is experiential learning whereby students and instructors work within their communities in ways that are related to their course material. This type of learning enhances students' academic skills, helps them develop a sense of civic responsibility, and encourages them to make the connection between theory and applications. To facilitate service-learning opportunities, many colleges offer their own initiatives, working with community leaders to battle hunger, illiteracy, and other social problems. These opportunities ensure that students further understand the parallels between the world of the classroom and the world at large.

In a UCLA study on service learning, Astin, Vogelgesang, Ikeda, and Yee (2000) looked specifically at the effect of community service and service learning on undergraduates; they found that service participation has a positive effect on students' academic performance, especially when the participation is associated with course-based service. In addition, students' leadership skills are enhanced through taking part in service learning. Besides increasing the level of engagement, service learning also helps students to achieve a greater awareness about the world and their role in it.

Besides college-wide initiatives, instructors in any number of courses can integrate elements of service and experiential learning into their classrooms. For instance, students in a developmental reading course might be assigned to visit a local elementary school and read with children or work as tutors at the local high school. Students in a photography course might create photo essays on hunger in America and display their results at a college-wide show, admission to which is a canned or nonperishable food item. There are countless ways to help students connect with their communities. Here are some examples:

- Students in computer classes might work with senior citizens or students in adult basic education programs. Students in a Web design course might work with a community group to develop a Web site.

- An accounting instructor might invite someone from a local nonprofit agency to speak to the class about the particular challenges that face nonprofits in the area of accounting. Students could then be asked to tackle some real-world business problems.

- Students in a forest ecology course might spend time volunteering at a state or local park. Park rangers or wildlife biologists might also present students with scenarios that depict their work with different constituents.

- Students enrolled in composition or business writing courses might help local agencies write press releases or help unemployed workers write cover letters.

- Algebra students could work with high school or junior high students to develop their skills in math.

- Students in a history course could interview residents in local nursing homes or veterans hospitals about their memories.

Whatever methods instructors use, it is important to implement opportunities for students to write about and discuss the experience in class. As with any other active-learning technique, students learn best from both participation and reflection.

Assessment and Evaluation

Effective instructors use a variety of assessment and evaluation techniques in their classes. In addition, colleges themselves may assess students' skills in specific areas and across the curriculum in order to gain understanding of students' needs and offer better support for the learning process. Feedback is essential to helping all of us grow in a teaching and learning institution.

In the classroom, assessment is often informal and anonymous. It may be a way for instructors to gauge the effectiveness of certain teaching methods or the absorption of specific content. Instructors provide students with questions or prompts in order to learn what they know and how they feel about it. Sometimes assessment is not anonymous, as when instructors observe students at work and respond accordingly. For instance, in a classroom or online discussion, instructors may point out insightful comments made by a particular student. Or an instructor may observe students at work during a small group exercise and offer immediate feedback on the performance.

Students may also provide feedback to other students. For example, after a student's presentation, the instructor may ask the class to describe at least one thing that was especially effective in the presentation. Students could also be asked to describe the speaker's main point. This anonymous feedback is then passed to the presenter. Many instructors also arrange for students to give peer feedback on final projects and papers. These kinds of assessment activities benefit more than the person who is receiving the feedback. A number of students find the process of assessing others' work especially helpful when it comes to completing their own projects.

Evaluation is a more formal way of measuring students' knowledge or skills. Although assessment techniques can be used spontaneously in the classroom, evaluation methods work best when thoughtfully planned and executed. After all, instructors should be sure their methods for evaluating students—exams, papers, presentations, or visual projects—are fair, balanced, and appropriate to the course. In addition, instructors should present students with clear expectations for the work they assign and how it will be evaluated. Because students are graded as a result of an instructor's evaluation methods, it is especially important to talk in some detail with students about the process.

For their part, students may assess and evaluate their course instruction. In the classroom, we can encourage students to assess us by providing them with multiple opportunities to complete "one-minute papers" (Cross & Angelo, 1988), questionnaires, and other forms of anonymous feedback during the course of the semester. In many colleges, students also formally evaluate their courses and instructors at the end. Besides rating their satisfaction with a course, students may evaluate certain priorities of the college community as a whole, such as those related to the institution's inclusiveness or the accessibility of instructors outside of class. Evaluation results may be compiled and made accessible to instructors in a printed or online format. Students at CCV complete a feedback form in each of their classes. The form is aligned with the college's Principles of Good Teaching and Learning, so instructors receive feedback on the goals and practices that have been established by the college. A copy of this form is provided in the appendix.

Although the feedback process can leave us feeling a little vulnerable, it is vital to the development of our courses. It may be best, in viewing student evaluations, to look for overall patterns rather than examples of isolated praise or complaint. Also, it may be helpful to look beyond the overall assessment of the course to the specific examples that students use to support their judgment. If a student indicates being satisfied with a course because of its lack of homework, it may represent an area of concern for the instructor. Whatever the feedback, instructors should take time to reflect on and use it to ask themselves some questions: What are their goals for the course and students? How does the feedback relate to these goals? How might they adapt the course and their instruction to address areas of concern or emphasize areas of strength?

College-Wide Assessment

Just as instructors measure how well individual students have achieved the objectives of their courses, community colleges are interested in how well students achieve the outcomes for their particular academic programs. Most colleges are invested in determining students' overall academic skills from the time they enter the classrooms to the time they graduate. Besides entrance assessments, which help students to be appropriately placed, many community colleges determine students' skills as they complete their programs. For instance, students graduating from St. Louis Community College are required to take part in an exit assessment that includes standardized testing. Depending on their academic or career area, they may also complete other assessments. Students at Valencia Community College (FL) must, prior to graduation, demonstrate proficiency in communication and computation through testing or alternate methods.

Instructors have a vital role in a college's assessment efforts, and the move to hold graduating students to standards is driven in part by instructors' commitment to teaching and evaluating the skills that will help students succeed in future education and work endeavors. Community college instructors, who often embody both theoretical knowledge and practical experience in the field, are particularly qualified to assist students in developing their academic and lifelong skills in learning.

Addressing Special Issues

Some of the issues instructors need to address in the classroom may not relate to the course content. These may be challenges associated with developing a classroom community, or a student's unique learning challenges. College students are individuals, and we should relate to them as such. At the same time, instructors must also consider the needs of the class. Balancing the needs of individual students with the needs of the class as a whole can be challenging. And yet, as with so many other aspects of teaching, when we reflect on our vision for a course, our goals for students, and our own values and experiences as instructors, we find that addressing classroom challenges can contribute to the growth and insight of everyone involved.

Diversity Issues

Community colleges have long embraced a commitment to access, which includes ensuring that equal access to the learning process is carried into the classroom environment. At the same time, community colleges cannot afford to be complacent; they must continue to articulate their values around inclusion. Community colleges recognize that they are not immune to the inequities in society and in the higher education environment.

Outright and subtle examples of gender, racial, ethnic, sexual orientation, age, religious, and socioeconomic class inequities are ubiquitous in college settings. In addition, sexual harassment, peer harassment, and unprofessional conduct between instructors and students have been problems in some colleges. Therefore, it is appropriate to raise everyone's consciousness about these issues so that we may become more sensitive and less likely to ignore or engage in them ourselves. The following are a few examples of inappropriate behaviors that have been reported in college settings.

- Inadvertently or purposefully excluding members of a particular racial, ethnic, religious, socioeconomic class, sexual orientation, or gender group from classroom activities.

- Allowing members of a particular racial, ethnic, religious, socioeconomic class, sexual orientation, or gender group to dominate classroom activities.

- Evaluating or assessing students in an inequitable manner on the basis of a student's race, ethnicity, religion, socioeconomic class, sexual orientation, or gender.

- Using images, humor, language, or examples that demean or degrade on the basis of sex, race, physical appearance, sexual orientation, socioeconomic class, or age.

- Touching students in ways that have sexual implications or any kind of touching not acceptable to the person involved.

Besides the issue of inequity, bias should also be a concern. It is important for instructors to be aware that many audiovisual and printed materials contain sexist, racist, ageist, or other stereotypical language. They may contain comments or illustrations that reflect a biased approach to the subject matter. For example, some texts completely ignore the contributions that women or ethnic minorities have made to a given discipline. Instructors should preview materials carefully and try to select those that do not contain these limitations. If instructors find it necessary to use materials that present a narrow or skewed approach to a subject, they should supplement these materials with others. In addition, they should address the limitations of the material with their class.

The Center for Teaching and Learning at the University of North Carolina at Chapel Hill (1997) has created a teaching handbook to address diversity in the college classroom. Although the handbook includes an entire chapter on strategies for inclusive teaching, it also begins by asking instructors to reflect on their own perceived diversity, both visible and invisible. As the authors of the handbook state, "The assumption that diversity has only to do with the students in the classroom can make it hard for a teacher to recognize personal hidden assumptions" (p. 4).

In addition to recognizing one's own differences and treating students as individuals, instructors can employ teaching strategies that help all students feel welcome in their classes. The following suggestions are adapted from the Center's handbook, *Teaching for Inclusion: Diversity in the College Classroom.*

■ Get to know students right away and create opportunities for them to get to know each other.

■ Ask students what their needs may be rather than making assumptions. In addition, regularly solicit students' feedback about the course and instruction through classroom assessment.

■ Establish a classroom atmosphere in which students feel it is safe to raise diverse opinions while still addressing injurious statements. One way of accomplishing this is through setting clear ground rules and developing shared goals for learning.

■ Encourage all students to participate in discussions from the beginning of the semester. Emphasize that all students have something important to contribute and act in ways that support this belief. Avoid ignoring or singling out students to speak on particular issues.

■ Depersonalize potentially controversial topics. For example, rather than asking students how they would respond to an ethical dilemma, an instructor might ask them to brainstorm on all the ways one could potentially respond to the dilemma.

Students With Disabilities

More students with disabilities enroll at community colleges than in other public higher education institutions, according to AACC. Community colleges provide a range of services, and many have designated programs that include strategies for success in the classroom and workplace. Lexington Community College (KY) has a disability support services office that offers a range of services to more than 500 students a year. In Maryland, Howard Community College's Project Access is designed to assist students with disabilities in facilitating their transition from high school to postsecondary education, increase their success rate and retention, and improve their career counseling and job placement. Longview Community College (MO) offers students with learning disabilities or brain injuries a support services program called ABLE (Academic Bridges to Learning Effectiveness). In the ABLE program, students enroll in a structured curriculum designed to help them succeed in college. In addition, the ABLE program includes a mentoring dimension that pairs former ABLE students with new students in the program.

In order for colleges to serve students with disabilities, students provide documentation and meet with appropriate college personnel so services can be arranged. Disability-related information is confidential, and the law prevents college personnel from sharing the nature of a student's disability with an instructor. An instructor does not need to know what the disability is, only that it has been appropriately verified by the individual assigned this responsibility on behalf of the institution and that accommodations have been determined.

Community colleges each have their own processes for contacting instructors. In general, an instructor receives notification from the college that a student should receive specific academic accommodations based on a documented disability. To make sure that both instructor and student are clear about how the accommodations will be implemented, the instructor discusses the matter with the student privately. The instructor should not ask the student to disclose the nature of the disability; the focus of the discussion should be on how the accommodations will be provided. If the instructor has questions regarding the accommodations, she or he should discuss them with appropriate college personnel.

If a student self-discloses that she or he has a disability, the instructor should refer the student to the appropriate staff member who will discuss the process for securing classroom accommodations—it is inappropriate for an instructor to determine an accommodation. As with other forms of diversity, instructors should avoid making assumptions about what students need or suggest to any student that she or he may have a disability.

In addition, we can help promote student success by employing teaching methods that make courses more accessible for all types of learners. These methods naturally incorporate the type of best practices that work well for many students with disabilities. Adapted from a Universal Design workshop presented by Megan Doney (2002) of Landmark College (VT), they include the following:

- Use advance organizers such as syllabi, weekly outlines, or daily plans for activities. These devices help adult learners prepare and focus on the upcoming academic work. Organizers also help motivate learners for the tasks ahead.

- Create activators such as case studies, scenarios, personal introductions, or lead-in questions. Activators help students create a personal connection with the material and give learners a way in to abstract concepts. These devices also help to encourage class participation.

- Provide clear directions and break down information into discrete, manageable chunks. Breaking information down helps students to begin the process of analyzing complex materials.

- Create connections between new and previous course content or skills. Connections such as this help students solidify connections in the material. Instructors can develop connections by linking the subject to other discipline areas or relating the content to the past, present, and future. Instructors can also help students create connections by asking them to imagine or use what if? statements.

- Use multisensory techniques in the class. Incorporating multisensory techniques is helpful in that it will encourage students to think in different ways. Instructors can do this by organizing information in a visual, kinesthetic, or auditory format. Also helpful is teaching to a variety of different learning styles and incorporating multiple intelligences theory.

- Build in time for strategizing and student reflection such as asking students to reflect on what worked and what did not with particular exercises or assignments. These devices allow students to reflect on their own work and to build a repertoire of strategies that do work. Reflecting also encourages metacognitive awareness for learners.

- Create ways for students to summarize what they have learned. These help learners to synthesize information and allow for incremental review of material toward a final goal.

- Develop routines for the class. Routines reduce memory load and language processing by way of distractions. This might be as simple as beginning every class with reaction writing and discussion.

- Allow for some choice and flexibility in assessment. For example, allowing students to demonstrate mastery or understanding in a variety of ways can elicit their best work and create an appreciation for diversity in the classroom.

In general, faculty and staff members can better serve students with disabilities by creating receptive classroom environments, being sensitive to their own language, promoting students' success, and adopting appropriate teaching and learning strategies (Prentice, 2002).

Learning Services

For many students, it takes a lot of courage to enroll in courses. They may be from the first generation in their families to go to college. In addition, many of them juggle work and family responsibilities in order to attend class. Their vision of a life richer in knowledge and opportunity is a tremendous motivator. Although the challenges associated with being underprepared for college can be daunting, students' connections to their institutions and learning environments can be a powerful element in their persistence. Research has illustrated that students "who are most involved with the college perceive that they are achieving" (Cohen & Brawer, 2003, p. 181).

Because so many community college students live off-campus, attend school part-time, and work, the classroom experience is the major institutional influence on them. This is one reason it is so important for instructors to create classroom communities in which students have the opportunity to develop as individuals and learners. In addition, community colleges offer the following range of activities and services to support and strengthen the classroom experience.

- Advising. The core of student service programs is academic advising or counseling. Advisors assist students with aspects of planning and carrying out their educational programs. In addition, advisors work with students to clarify and achieve their goals.

- Entrance assessments. Proficiency in the basic skills of reading, writing, and math is crucial to students' academic success. Entrance assessments help academic advisors and students determine the most appropriate courses for enrollment.

- Developmental skills programs. Assessment results may indicate that a student is not ready for college-level course work. Many students need to start with one or two foundational courses to help them develop or strengthen the necessary skills for successful college work.

- Freshman orientation seminars. In their efforts to increase engagement and retention, institutions have developed ways to effectively introduce students to the college experience. Freshman orientations include opportunities to develop critical skills, establish faculty and peer relationships, and become familiar with the academic culture. Orientations may be packaged as seminars, workshops, or courses.

- Learning assistance centers. Sometimes referred to as learning labs or learning centers, community colleges provide students with the opportunity to receive assistance with their academic work. Some learning centers include testing services, developmental skills courses, and advising assistance. Other learning centers include programs designed to help students improve their writing, math, computer, English-as-a-second-language, and study skills. Students may work on these skills one-on-one with specially trained instructors, peer tutors, or online instructors.

- Federal and state grant programs offering student support services. In addition to the various services offered through institutional support, many community colleges receive federal and state grants to provide services to students. The TRIO program is designed to increase the academic success, retention, graduation, and transfer rates of eligible students by helping them develop the skills to become successful in their college course work. TRIO/Student Support Services helps qualified students through intensive advising, labs, tutoring, developmental skills course work, career planning, transfer counseling, and other individualized assistance.

- Transfer programs. For many students, enrollment in a community college is a stepping-stone to a bachelor's degree. However, receiving institutions still have their own policies and usually determine which credits may be transferred and how they count toward their requirements. As a result, community colleges work actively to develop and maintain formal articulation agreements with universities and other colleges. Some agreements offer students financial incentives; others include guaranteed admission and course equivalencies. Transfer programs work not only with students in their transition from community colleges, but also with high school and other students in easing their transition to community colleges.

- Career development. Career development is another way in which community colleges address the needs of the whole student or learner. These services assist students with self-assessment, exploration, and decision making with the goals of helping students understand the career development process and locate resources within their communities throughout their adult lives. Career development may take the shape of specialized courses, as in the case of internships, or be embedded within courses. In fact, one of the best places for career exploration is in the classroom. Instructors play an essential role in the process by serving as role models and mentors. Furthermore, instructors can help students develop these necessary skills by making connections between their classroom learning experience and their career goals.

It is important that instructors know which services are available to their students and support their usage. According to Cohen and Brawer (2003), "when special treatment is applied; when students are given supplemental counseling, tutoring and learning aides; and they are singled out for additional work, they tend to remain in school" (p. 267). If we want to best serve students, we must engage them as learners both in and out of the classroom.

Conclusion

Excellent instructors come in all varieties. There is, in fact, no stereotypical great teacher. But some characteristics are common among most successful instructors. For one thing, they have a solid grasp of their subject and can present it in a clear, simple, and articulate manner using active learning techniques to engage students. Another quality present in many good instructors is enthusiasm for the subject, especially when that enthusiasm is combined with real sensitivity to student needs and genuine concern for their development.

Even if we initially struggle in certain aspects of teaching, we can—through assessment and practice—develop our skills. After all, we encourage students to take risks in their learning and support them through the process; why should we not give ourselves the same opportunities for growth? The idea that good teachers are born with special talents is probably a partial truth at best. Even those of us who feel innately suited to the classroom must work against a sense of complacency. Only through challenging ourselves do we model the kinds of risk inherent in learning.

The idea that good teachers are born with special talents is probably a partial truth at best. Even those of us who feel innately suited to the classroom must work against a sense of complacency. Only through challenging ourselves do we model the kinds of risk inherent in learning.

Powell (2002) drew on her experience as a poet to inform her work as a teacher. She is useful as a guide because the poet is not afraid of false starts or detours, is slower and more attuned to the rhythms around, embraces questions, and is drawn inward. From my own experience, the poet must also be wary of going through the motions. Poetry, like teaching, demands a degree of mindfulness. In addition, Powell saw a connection between the poet and teacher as conduit: "What she believes in; what she understands about human development, the arts, and the human spirit; and what she will allow to flow through her, are crucial to the success of education" (p. 352).

Whether we call forward our inner poet, artist, scientist, or manager, the simple act of reflecting is a powerful step toward realizing our potential as a teacher (not that this process will ever be completed). Every time we step into a classroom, physical or virtual, we have the opportunity to see ourselves and others anew. And as long as there are students with whom to collaborate, teaching will always embody both risk and reward.

References

American Association of Community Colleges. (2001). *America's community colleges: A century of innovation.* (2001). Washington, DC: Community College Press.

Andrews, H. A. (2001). *The dual-credit phenomenon: Challenging secondary school students across 50 states.* Stillwater, OK: New Forums Press. (ERIC No. ED 463 823)

Andrews, H. A. (2003). *Enrollment trends in community colleges.* Los Angeles, CA: ERIC Clearinghouse for Community Colleges. (ERIC No. EDO-JC-0305)

Astin, A. W., Vogelgesang, L. J., Ikeda, E. K., & Yee, J. A. (2000). *How service learning affects students.* Los Angeles: UCLA Graduate School of Education and Information Studies, University of California Higher Education Research Institute.

Bailey, T. R., & Averianova, I. E. (1999, May). Multiple missions of community colleges: Conflicting or complementary? *Community College Research Center Brief, 1,* 1–6.

Belenky, M. F., Clinchy, B. M., Goldberger, M. R., & Tarule, J. M. (1986). *Women's ways of knowing: The development of self, voice, and mind* (2nd ed.). New York: Basic Books.

Bloom, B. (1956). *Taxonomy of educational objectives: Cognitive domain.* New York: David McKay.

Blythe, H., & Sweet, C. (2003, November). Five more ways sports coaches model good instruction. *The Teaching Professor, 17*(9), 5.

Boyd, R. D. (1991). *Personal transformations in small groups: A Jungian perspective.* London: Routledge.

Briggs, K. C., & Myers, I. B. (1977). *Myers-Briggs type indicator.* Palo Alto, CA: Consulting Psychologists Press.

Brookfield, S. D. (1987). Developing critical thinkers: *Challenging adults to explore alternative ways of thinking and acting.* San Francisco: Jossey-Bass.

Center for Teaching and Learning at University of North Carolina at Chapel Hill. (1997). *Teaching for inclusion: Diversity in the college classroom.* Chapel Hill, NC: Author.

Chickering, A. W., & Ehrmann, S. (1996, October). Implementing the seven principles: Technology as lever. *AAHE Bulletin,* 3–6.

Chickering, A. W., & Gamson, Z. (1987, March). Seven principles for good practice in undergraduate education. *AAHE Bulletin.* Retrieved February 16, 2004, from http://learningcommons.evergreen.edu/pdf/fall1987.pdf

Cohen, A. M. (1993). *General education in community colleges.* Los Angeles: ERIC Clearinghouse for Community Colleges. (ERIC No. ED 362 253)

Cohen, A. M., & Brawer, F. B. (2003). *The American community college* (4th ed.). San Francisco: Jossey-Bass.

Coley, R. J. (2000). *The American community college turns 100: A look at its students, programs, and prospects.* Princeton, NJ: Educational Testing Service.

Cranton, P. (1994). *Understanding and promoting transformative learning: A guide for educators of adults.* San Francisco: Jossey-Bass.

Cross, K. P., & Angelo, T. (1988). *Classroom assessment techniques: A handbook for faculty.* Ann Arbor, MI: University of Michigan, National Center for Research to Improve Postsecondary Teaching and Learning.

Daloz, L. A. (1986). *Effective teaching and mentoring: Realizing the transformational power of adult learning experiences.* San Francisco: Jossey-Bass.

Davis, B. G. (1993). *Tools for teaching.* San Francisco: Jossey-Bass.

Doney, M. (2002, April 27). *The principles of universal design.* Paper presented at the Instructor Development Conference, Community College of Vermont at Vermont Technical College, Randolph.

Duncombe, S., & Heikkinen, M. H. (1988, Winter). Role playing for different viewpoints. *College Teaching, 36*(1), 3–5.

Eble, K. (1977). *The craft of teaching: A guide to mastering the professor's art.* San Francisco: Jossey-Bass.

Entwhistle, N. J. (1988). *Styles of learning and teaching.* London: David Fulton.

Fulwiler, T. (1982). The personal connection: Journal writing across the curriculum. In T. Fulwiler & A. Young (Eds.) *Language connections: Writing and reading across the curriculum* (pp. 15–31). Urbana, IL: National Council of Teachers of English.

Gardner, H. (1983). *Frames of mind.* New York: Basic Books.

Gardner, H. (1993). *Multiple intelligences: The theory in practice.* New York: Basic Books.

Golding, T. L., & Weimer, M. (2004, January). Working in groups—understanding but not applying. *The Teaching Professor, 18*(1), 1, 4.

Harris, T. (2004, January 6). More remedial study done at 2-year colleges. *Community College Times.* Retrieved January 14, 2004, from http://www.aacc.nche.edu

Herreid, C. F. (1997, December/1998, January). What makes a good case? *Journal of College Science Teaching,* 163–165.

Hesse, M. (1980). *Revolutions and reconstructions in the philosophy of science.* Bloomington, IN: Indiana University Press.

Hurst, D. & Smerdon, B. (2000, June). *Post-secondary students with disabilities: Enrollment, services, and persistence* (Stats in brief) (NCES 2000-92). Washington, DC: U.S. Department of Education, National Center for Educational Statistics.

Johnson, S. D., & Benson, A. D. (2003, October). *Distance learning in postsecondary career and technical education.* St. Paul, MN: National Research Center for Career and Technical Education.

Johnston, G. R. (1988). *Taking teaching seriously: A faculty handbook.* College Station: Texas A&M University Center for Teaching Excellence.

Klein, G. S., Riley, W. G., & Schlesinger, H. G. (1962). Tolerance for unrealistic experience: A study of the generality of cognitive control. *British Journal of Psychology, 54,* 41–55.

Kloss, R. (1987, Fall). Coaching and playing right field: Trying on metaphors for teaching. *College Teaching, 35*(4), 134–139.

Kolb, D. A. (1984). *Experiential learning: Experience as the source of learning and development.* Englewood Cliffs, NJ: Prentice Hall.

Kolb, D. A., & Fry, R. (1975). Toward an applied theory of experiential learning. In C. Cooper (Ed.), *Theories of group process* (pp. 33–57). New York: Wiley.

Marini, Z. (2000, April). The teacher as a Sherpa guide. *The Teaching Professor, 14*(4), 5.

Martin, E. (1999). *Changing academic work: Developing the learning university.* Philadelphia:

The Society for Research into Higher Education and Open University Press.

McCarthy, B. (1996). *About learning*. Wauconda, IL: About Learning, Inc.

McCarthy, B. (2000). *About teaching: 4MAT in the classroom*. Wauconda, IL: About Learning, Inc.

McKeachie, W. J. (1978). *Teaching tips: A guidebook for the beginning college teacher*. Lexington, MA: DC Heath.

Mellert, R. B. (1998, August). *Searching for the foundations of Whitehead's philosophy of education*. Paper presented at the 1998 Twentieth World Congress of Philosophy. Retrieved February 27, 2004, from http://www.bu.edu/wcp/Papers/Educ/EducMell.htm

Mezirow, J. (1991). *Transformative dimensions of adult learning*. San Francisco: Jossey-Bass.

Mezirow, J. (1997, Summer). Transformative learning: Theory to practice. In P. Cranton (Ed.), *Transformative learning in action: Insights from practice* (pp. 5–12). Directions for Adult and Continuing Education No. 74. San Francisco: Jossey-Bass.

Moore, W. S. (n.d.). "My mind exploded": Intellectual development as a critical framework for understanding and assessing collaborative learning. In Washington Center Evaluation Committee (Ed.), *Assessment in and of collaborative learning: Handbook*. Retrieved March 2, 2004, from www.evergreen.edu/washcenter/resources/acl/iia.html

National Center for Educational Statistics (2003). *Digest of educational statistics 2002* (NCES 2003-060, Table 250). Washington, DC: U.S. Department of Education.

National Training Laboratories. (n.d.). Learning pyramid. In *Master teacher: Active learning strategies*. Retrieved February 20, 2004, from http://www.accd.edu/spc/iic/master/active.htm

Nodding, N. (1995). *Philosophy of education*. Boulder, CO: Westview Press.

O'Banion, T. (1997). *Creating more learning-centered community colleges*. Mission Viejo, CA: League for Innovation in the Community College.

Palmer, P. (1997). *The courage to teach: Exploring the inner landscape of a teacher's life*. San Francisco: Jossey-Bass.

Palmer, P. (1999, January). *Good talk about good teaching: Improving teaching through conversation and community*. Retrieved February 18, 2004, from http://www.mcli.dist.maricopa.edu/events/afc99/articles/goodtalk.html

Parrott, S. (1995). *Future learning: Distance education in community colleges*. Los Angeles: ERIC Clearinghouse for Community Colleges. (ERIC No. ED 385 311)

Peirce, W. (2001). Strategies for teaching thinking and promoting intellectual development in online classes. In S. Reisman (Ed.), *Electronic communities: Current issues and best practices*. Retrieved March 2, 2004, from http://academic.pg.cc.md.us/~wpeirce/MCCCTR/ttol.html

Perry, W. G. (1999). *Forms of intellectual and ethical development in the college years: A scheme*. San Francisco: Jossey-Bass.

Phillippe, K. A., & Patton, M. (2000). *National profile of community colleges: Trends and statistics* (3rd ed.). Washington, DC: Community College Press. (*Note*. A new edition was in preparation as of July 2004.)

Powell, M. C. (2002). Why I send the poet to teach my courses. In E. Mirochnik & D. Sherman (Eds.), Passion and pedagogy: *Relation, creation, and transformation in teaching*. New York: Peter Lang.

Prentice, M. (2002). *Serving students with disabilities at the community college.* Los Angeles, CA: ERIC Clearinghouse for Community Colleges. (ERIC No. EDO-JC-0202)

Rayner, S., & Riding, R. (1997, March/June). Toward a categorization of cognitive style and learning style. *Educational psychology, 17*(1/2), 5–28.

Rodgers, C. (1969). *Freedom to learn.* Upper Saddle River, NJ: Merrill/Prentice Hall.

Rose, M. (1989). *Lives on the boundary: A moving account of the struggles and achievements of America's educationally underprepared.* New York: Penguin Books.

Sheckley, B. G. (1984). The adult as learner: A case for making higher education more responsive to the individual learner. *CAEL News,* 7–8.

Shor, I. (1980). *Critical teaching and everyday life.* Boston: South End Press.

Shults, C. (2000). *Remedial education: Practices and policies in community colleges.* Washington, DC: Community College Press.

Soven, M. (1988). Beyond the first workshop: What else can you do to help faculty? In S. H. McLeod (Ed.), *Strengthening programs for writing across the curriculum* (pp. 13–20). San Francisco: Jossey-Bass.

Steitz, J. A. (1985). Issues of adult development within the academic environment. *Lifelong Learning,* 15–18, 27.

Stout, B. R., & Magnotto, J. N. (1988). Writing across the curriculum at community colleges. In S. H. McLeod (Ed.), *Strengthening programs for writing across the curriculum* (pp. 21–30). San Francisco: Jossey-Bass.

Striplin, J. C. (2000). *A review of community college curriculum trends.* Los Angeles, CA: ERIC Clearinghouse for Community Colleges. (ERIC No. ED 438 011)

Surrey, J. L. (1991). The self-in-relation: A theory of women's development. In J. Jordan, A. G. Kaplan, J. B. Miller, I. P. Stiver, & J. L. Surrey (Eds.), *Women's growth in connection, writings from the stone center.* New York: Guilford Press.

Taylor, K., Marienau, C., & Fiddler, M. (2000). *Developing adult learners: Strategies for teachers and trainers.* San Francisco: Jossey-Bass.

Vermont High School Task Force. (2002). *High Schools on the move: Renewing Vermont's commitment to quality secondary education.* Montpelier: Vermont Department of Education.

Waits, T., & Lewis, L. (2003). *Distance education at degree-granting postsecondary institutions: 2000–2001.* (NCES 2003017). Washington, DC: U.S. Department of Education, National Center for Education Statistics.

Weinstein, P. (1999, November). Jazz teaching: The metaphor is the method. *The Teaching Professor, 13*(9), 6.

Werner, R. E. (2000, November). *A matrix for course planning.* Paper presented at the Instructor Development Conference on Teaching and Learning, Community College of Vermont, Montpelier.

Witkin, H. A., & Goodenough, D. (1981). *Cognitive styles, essence and origins: Field dependence and field independence.* New York: International Universities Press.

Young, A. (1982). Considering values: The poetic function of language. In T. Fulwiler & A. Young (Eds.), *Language connections: Writing and reading across the curriculum* (pp. 77–97). Urbana, IL: National Council of Teachers of English.

Appendix: Resources for Instructors

Whether we are teaching our first semester or our 14th, we can all benefit from thinking about our needs as instructors. We might have specific needs related to designing a new course or we might be interested in exploring different ways to engage our students. We could be looking for teaching resources that will help to sustain us or those that will help to move us out of our comfort zones. Whatever we are looking for, today more than ever, resources are available—books, journals, Web sites, you name it. But for many, our richest resource can be found in each other: conversations down the hall and across the world. This appendix contains a few basic tools for developing a course's architecture, reflecting on the readiness to teach, and thinking about your values as an instructor.

Sample Syllabi

Microcomputer Applications I
Fall 2001
Instructor: Jane Doe
doejane@communitycollege.edu

This course is a hands-on introduction to information processing using operating system and application software designed for microcomputers. Covers file management, Windows, word processing, and spreadsheets. Recommended prior learning: keyboarding skills and basic algebra.

LEARNING OBJECTIVES:

The successful student will be able to:

1. Describe the hardware components of a computer system and explain how they work together.

2. Describe the general functions of the operating system and its interaction with computer hardware and applications software.

3. Describe the significance and threat of computer viruses and have an understanding of the need for and the current methods of file backup procedures.

4. Explain the function and demonstrate the primary features of the Windows environment, including essential file management procedures, data transfer within and between documents and applications, adding program icons and group windows, using the print manager, customizing the Windows display, configuring printers and controlling mouse operations, and use the common Windows accessories such as Notepad and Paintbrush.

5. Explain the function and primary features of a word processing program. Compose, modify, format, spell check, print, save, and retrieve documents using a word processing program. Also apply other generally available special features.

6. Explain the function and primary features of a spreadsheet program. Design and build a spreadsheet using labels, values, formulas, functions, and differentiating between absolute and relative references. Modify a spreadsheet using various copying and formatting options. Save, print and retrieve a spreadsheet. Build and print a graph/chart.

7. Identify and understand the appropriate uses of these software applications in the work environment.

8. Discuss legal and ethical issues related to computers and information processing.

METHODS:

1. Class discussion
2. Tutorials and practice
3. In-class activities and projects
4. Presentations

EVALUATION:

The student's grade will be based on the following criteria:
1. Attendance and class participation—20%
2. Quizzes—20%
3. Homework—25%
4. Tests—15%
5. Projects and presentations—20%

TEXTS:

MS Excel 2000, Shelly, Cashman & Quasney; Course technology, 2000.
MS Word 2000, Shelly, Cashman & Vermaat; Course technology, 2000.

GRADE CRITERIA:

A+ THROUGH A- Superior work that reveals a thorough understanding of all course concepts and objectives. Assignments will be nearly error-free. Quizzes, homework, and projects will have grades 90%–100%.

B+ THROUGH B- Above average work that shows a good understanding of all course objectives and concepts. Assignments will have few errors or omissions. Quizzes, homework, and projects will have grades 80%–89.9%.

C+ THROUGH C- Satisfactory work that demonstrates comprehension of the course concepts and objectives, but with evidence of factual, format, or organizational errors/omissions. Quizzes, homework, and projects will have grades 70%–79.9%.

D+ THROUGH D- Weak work that only marginally demonstrates comprehension of course concepts and objectives. Quizzes, homework, and projects will have grades 60%–69.9%.

F Unsatisfactory work that reveals obvious deficiencies of fact or formatting or is incomplete to the extent that no credit can be given. Quizzes, homework, and projects will have grades below 60%.

OUTLINE OF COURSE ACTIVITIES & ASSIGNMENTS:

Class 1: September XX
■ Course overview, including: syllabus, course description, class expectations, grading, and assignments
■ Introductions and class activity
■ Review of computer components and general terminology
■ Discussion of Windows Operating System — Project 1
■ Begin Project 1: *Fundamentals of Using Windows*, pp. WIN1.4–WIN1.54

Homework:
■ Read *Introduction to Using Computers*, handout
■ Answer Questions on handout, *Micro Apps 1 Student Assignment Week 1*
■ Complete Project 1: *Fundamentals of Using Windows*, pp. WIN1.6–WIN1.51
■ Do *Test Your Knowledge* #1, #2 and #3, pp. WIN1.52–WIN1.54
■ Do *In the Lab* #4, p. WIN1.62

Class 2: September XX

- Review homework
- Discuss Bitmap images
- Class activity and discussion of Project 2:
- Begin Project 2: *Working on and Modifying the Windows Desktop*, pp. WIN2.4–WIN2.63 (work independently or in groups)

Homework:
- Complete Project 2, pp. WIN2.4 – WIN2.63
- Create a Bitmap image map to your house, place of work, favorite restaurant or store or other location of your choosing. The map must include a title, a key, road names, buildings and at least four colors.
- Do *Test Your Knowledge* #1 and #2, pp. WIN2.64–WIN2.65
- Do *In the Lab* #1, #2, and #3, pp. WIN2.72–WIN2.76
- Do *Cases and Places* #1, pp. WIN2.79
- Other_____

Class 3: September XX
- Review homework
- Class activity and discussion of Project 3
- Review for next week's quiz
- Begin Project 3: *File Document and Folder Management*, pp. WIN3.4–WIN3.58 (work independently or in groups)

Homework:
- Complete Project 3, pp. WIN3.4–WIN3.58
- Do *Test Your Knowledge* #1 and #2, pp. 3.54–3.55
- Do *In the Lab* #2, pp. 3.60–3.61
- Do *Cases and Places* #1, p. 3.63
- Study for quiz #1
- Other_____

SUPPLEMENTARY INFORMATION FOR THIS COURSE:

- Homework will be collected and graded using a √+, √, √-, 0 system. Please print all homework and save it to a disk.

- Homework will be accepted up to one week late, but no later. All late homework will be marked down one grade. Homework that is completed in class on the day it is due will be considered late.

- Quizzes cannot be made up. However, the lowest quiz score will be dropped from your final grade. In the event that you miss a quiz, that score will be dropped.

- Should you be absent on the day of the mid-term, final exam, or final presentation, you may jeopardize your grade in the course. Special arrangements and permission of the instructor must be made in order to make up any of these assignments.

- Three or more absences will put you at serious risk for failing the class.

- Additional grading policies and procedures relating to activities, projects, and presentations will be discussed in class.

Mythology
Fall 2003
Instructor: John Doe
doejohn@communitycollege.edu

This course is an exploration of the meaning of mythology and the evolution of mythical thought from an inter-disciplinary standpoint. Consideration will be given to mythology as an explanation of the way the world is ordered and how human beings respond to that order. The course will examine the relevance of myths in our daily lives.

Throughout the semester, we'll explore important themes in world mythology, such as those associated with creation, death, tricksters, quests, goddesses and gods, and sacred places. Although our main focus will be the myths themselves, we'll also explore the historical, social, and cultural contexts of myths, including the ways artists and poets have used myth to shape their work. Because the best way to understand and appreciate mythology is to be fully engaged with it, we will do a variety of hands-on activities in class to promote learning. Therefore, it is important for you to attend class and come prepared.

Course Goals:

1. Examine myths from the perspective of a variety of disciplines;

2. Compare and contrast different cultural approaches to myth while recognizing the universality of mythical themes;

3. Analyze the connection between myths and human development;

4. Compare and contrast the journeys of heroines and heroes;

5. Examine cultural paradigms and explain how myths can define a culture's ideals;

6. Interpret mythical images, themes, and archetypes in written works and in art forms;

7. Determine the relevance and importance of myths in our modern world and in the student's personal development.

Class Meeting Dates & Times:

Class will meet every Tuesday 9 a.m.–12. p.m. beginning September 2 and ending December 9.

Instructor Contact Information:

Phone number: 888-555-1111
Email address: doejohn@communitycollege.edu
Office Hours: Tuesdays after class, Thursdays 9–12

TEXTS:

- Leonard, Scott and Michael McClure
  Myth & Knowing: An Introduction to World Mythology, Boston: McGraw Hill, 2004

- Campbell, Joseph with Bill Moyers
  The Power of Myth, New York: Anchor, 1988

- Assorted other readings are available online

METHODS:

Small-group and whole-group discussion
Mini-lecture
Small group activities, including games and simulations
In-class reaction writing and other writing assignments
Extra-credit quizzes to build comprehension and analysis
Midterm and final exams
Student presentations
Research project on topic of student's choosing

MEANS OF EVALUATION:

Homework: 15%
Participation and attendance (includes being prepared for class): 10%
Final research paper: 20%
Oral presentation with annotated bibliography: 20%
Midterm and final exams: 35%

GRADE CRITERIA:

For any work to receive an "A," it must clearly be exceptional or outstanding work. It must demonstrate keen insight and original thinking. It must not only demonstrate full understanding of the topic or issues addressed, but it must also provide a critical analysis of these. In addition, an "A" grade reflects a student's ability to clearly and thoughtfully articulate his or her learning.

For any work to receive a "B," it must be good-to-excellent work. It must demonstrate strong originality, comprehension, critical thinking, and attention to detail. In addition, a "B" grade reflects a student's ability to clearly articulate his or her learning.

For any work to receive a "C," it must meet the expectations of the assignment. It must demonstrate solid comprehension, critical thinking, and attention to detail. In addition, a "C" grade reflects a student's ability to adequately articulate his or her learning.

For any work to receive a "D," it must marginally meet the expectations of the assignment. It must demonstrate at least some comprehension, critical thinking, and attention to detail. In addition, a "D" grade may reflect a student's difficulty in articulating his or her learning.

Work that receives an "F" grade does not meet the expectations or objectives of the assignment. It demonstrates consistent problems with comprehension, organization, critical thinking, and supporting details. In addition, an "F" grade reflects a student's inability to articulate his or her learning.

Course Outline:

September 2: Mythology & Human Development

Topics & Activities: Introduction to the course and mythology, Hominid Evolution, Burial Customs and Graves

Homework:
- Read pages 32–46 of Chapter 2 in *Myth & Knowing (M & K)* on types of creation myths, and then read the Dogon (p. 46), Norse (p. 58), Iroquois (p. 68), Genesis (p. 84), and Maya (p. 90) myths.
- Read "The First Storytellers" in Campbell's *Power of Myth (P of M)*.
- Complete a response essay (double-spaced, 3–5 pages)—See Guidelines and Topic Choices

September 9: Creation Myths

Topics & Activities: Symbols, Relationships between humans and deities, The role of animals, Speech and language in creation stories

Homework:
- Read pages 102–122 of Chapter 3 in *M & K* on the female divine, and then read the Hawaiian (p. 122), Sioux (p132), Sumerian (p. 137), and Vietnamese (p144) myths.
- Read "The Gift of the Goddess" in Campbell's *Power of Myth (P of M)*.
- Complete a response essay (double-spaced, 3–5 pages)—See Guidelines and Topic Choices

SUPPLEMENTARY INFORMATION: IMPORTANT THINGS FOR YOU TO KNOW

Late work will be penalized. You must turn in homework and other assignments by Friday of the week it is due, if you wish to receive any credit. This is true whether or not you attend class. You may drop work off at my college mailbox or you may e-mail it to me.

You must attend class. The activities we do in class are important in helping you to meet the goals of this course. Homework will not make up for lack of attendance. You cannot expect to pass this course if you miss more than three classes. Please notify me if you are going to be absent from class.

This course covers a lot of material. In order to participate fully in classroom activities, you must come prepared. This means that you need to have completed your assigned reading and writing when you come to class. If you have difficulty with an assignment, you should contact me between class sessions. You also should note your difficulties, questions, or frustrations in your academic journals. These can be great discussion starters for the class. In fact, I will often ask you to contribute questions and comments anonymously at the beginning of the class just for this purpose.

There will be exams and quizzes to assess your knowledge. However, the purpose of my exams is not to trick you or discover the cracks in your knowledge. The midterm and final exams are designed as learning tools as well as evaluative tools. Each exam will offer you a choice of questions. At the end of each exam, I will be asking for anonymous feedback on the exam itself. During the semester, there will also be unannounced or pop quizzes. These are extra-credit opportunities for students to assess their learning in a test format. If students do better than 85 percent on the quiz, they will gain extra credit points toward the homework portion of their final grades. If students perform less than 85 percent on the quizzes, they will receive no extra credit.

Syllabus Template

COURSE TITLE: *Standard title and course code.*

INSTRUCTOR: *Your name and contact information (e-mail address, phone, office hours).*

DAY/TIME & TERM: *When the course meets and for how long.*

COURSE DESCRIPTION: *Catalog description of the course.*

LEARNING OBJECTIVES: *Your goals for the course. The college's goals for the course, if articulated. Think about what the successful student will be able to do as a result of completing the course.*

TEXTBOOK: *Provide all the information about required text(s), including ISBN.*

METHODS: *The kinds of methods you will use to teach the course. The kinds of activities students will be expected to undertake in the classroom.*

EVALUATION: *Your evaluation methods. An explanation of how a student's final grade will be tabulated (e.g., two exams worth 30 percent). May include letter grade criteria.*

OUTLINE OF COURSE MEETINGS & ASSIGNMENTS: *Breakdown of course topics and assignments by date. Especially useful for noting significant dates, such as those associated with exams, projects, or presentations.*

COURSE PHILOSOPHY: *An opportunity for you to address your interest in or experience with the subject, as well as your philosophy in teaching the subject. For example, you might address the importance of writing and critical thinking skills in your course.*

ATTENDANCE AND OTHER POLICIES: *Outline your policy on missing class and arriving late/leaving early. Also, how will you respond to late assignments?*

ACADEMIC HONESTY: *Your expectations for student conduct around assignments and exams can be described here.*

Sample Lesson Plan

_____

**Autobiography & Memoir
Class 1: June 7**

A. ICEBREAKER: GETTING TO KNOW EACH OTHER (ALLOW 30 MINUTES)

Explain to students that we're going to start the course by playing a game that helps us get to know each other a little better and generates some ideas for future writing. Give each student a bingo card and go over the directions.

Students collect a name or signature from each student in the class on one of the squares on their card (e.g., one square might read: knows three languages). When students have a signature/name from every other student in the class, they can go back and get peers to sign off on additional squares. The first student to get a bingo yells out, and his or her card is verified.

After the game, explain that this is a fun way to get to know each other, but it also goes to show that we all have many different topics available to us for writing our memoirs.

B. SYLLABUS, EXPECTATIONS, COURSE PHILOSOPHY, AND OTHER ISSUES (ALLOW 30–45 MINUTES)

Spend time going over the syllabus and structure of the course. Talk about the expectations for homework and attendance, including reading logs. Finally, describe the philosophy of the course (writing and sharing of memories requires confidentiality and respect for each other). Be sure to give copy of the rubric also.

[Break: 10–15 minutes]

C. LOOKING FOR THEMES (ALLOW 30–45 MINUTES)

1. Split students into groups.
2. Give each group a packet of photos to look at.
3. Ask students to arrange the photos in some order using some type of principle.
4. When students have done this, ask them to report on how they organized the photos (e.g., historical time, life-span development, etc.). Write this on the board. Ask students to organize them again, using a different principle—one not mentioned. Repeat process a total of three times.
   Purpose: What distinguishes memoir from autobiography is precisely this kind of shaping or organizing of our memories, and one can see by this exercise that there are many ways to tell or shape a story. Autobiography moves in a linear fashion, although the writer must decide what to leave in or take out. Memoir tries to find a theme or organizing principle to our life's story.
5. Give handout on types of autobiographical writing.
6. Now ask students to each select one photo out of the packet, a photo that that is compelling to them in some way. (Students should go back to their own seats for this part of the exercise). Using that photo, have each student write a first-person (define this on the board) narrative in the voice of a character from that photo. Describe the circumstances or story behind the photo, imagine the relationships the character has with the others in the photo, if there are others. Share with the rest of the class.
   Purpose: We need to use imagination even in developing our own stories, our own voices. It is important to invent the truth where we can't remember it. This does not mean that we should be reckless or careless about the truth; it means that too much reliance on the facts can make a piece of writing lifeless and dull. All memoir writers need to strive for an emotional or authentic truth, a resonance that feels true to memory.

There's a responsibility in this not to misuse our imagination or misrepresent people in order to get revenge or make ourselves look better than we are. But in early drafts especially, it's important to be freer with our imagination.

D. CREATING A WORD LIST (ALLOW 45 MINUTES)

Words and images can instantly transport us back in time. They can help us generate ideas, topics, and even memories we've lost or put aside. We tend to remember big events, but forget the small, often powerful and evocative ones. This exercise may help you find those memories or sensations.

To create the word list:

1. write down the first word you think of when I say "rain"
2. the city/town where you were born
3. the first word that comes to mind when I say "justice"
4. the place you'd most like to be right now
5. your favorite color
6. your least favorite color
7. the word you think of when I say "whispering"
8. the first word…"dim"
9. the first word…"secret"
10. the word "mutt"
11. the word "avenue"
12. the first word…"watercolors"
13. the first word…"swoop"
14. the word "pear"
15. the word "rain"
16. the word "tangled"
17. the first word…"field"
18. the first word…"blustery"
19. the word "chain"
20. the name of the first street you can remember living on
21. the word "orange"
22. your favorite season
23. one particular characteristic of that season
24. the word "pencil"
25. the first word… "kitchen"
26. the word "pigeon"
27. the word "maple"
28. the word "cello"
29. the word "torn"
30. the word "catapulted"
31. the name of your least favorite season
32. one particular characteristic of that season
33. the word "neck"
34. the word "grace"
35. the word "awkward"
36. the first word…"broken"

37. the first word ... "first grade"
38. the first word... "mother"
39. the word "window"
40. the first word... "journey"

Now, cross out any ten words. Pause a moment and cross out another ten. Now write using as many words as you can from your remaining list. No special order, no special topic. Don't even worry about making sense. Just write, getting as many words into the writing as you can.

Write for about 20 minutes or so, and then ask for volunteers to share.

E. REVIEW HOMEWORK

- Read Stephen Kuusisto's *Planet of the Blind*
- Complete reading log
- Choose one of the memoir pieces you began in class (could be for brainstorming exercise or free-writing exercise) and create a 2–3 page typed draft. *(Note: We will be working with these in class and sharing them with each other).*

Sample Rubrics

Rubrics are powerful tools for teaching and learning. Not only can instructors use them to clarify their expectations for an assignment, they may involve students in the making of the rubrics. The class can work together to decide how an assignment should be evaluated and what distinguishes a strong and effective reaction paper, for example, from a weak one. Rubrics also have been used successfully in math and science courses, among others, to evaluate students' problem-solving skills, lab reports, and other assignments. Some online instructors use rubrics to evaluate students' asynchronous discussion contributions. This helps both students and instructors construct the most meaningful discussions possible each week.

When creating rubrics, it is useful to begin by thinking about the assignment and what you want students to be able to demonstrate as a result. Try to capture the most essential objectives associated with the assignment; of course, these should be brief, descriptive, and measurable. In fact, some of a rubric's greatest power comes from its concrete description of what is abstract and amorphous. Once a rubric is created, test it with hypothetical cases. What kinds of work might you receive from students? How would this work be evaluated in terms of the rubric? Again, when possible, students should be involved, because, for evaluation to be most effective, students should have some ownership in the process. The following are sample rubrics that have been developed for general writing assignments, oral presentations, and research papers.

	EXCELLENT	**GOOD**	**FAIR**	**WEAK**
FOCUS	Clear, central thesis & purpose; addresses all aspects of thesis	Clear, central thesis & purpose; addresses most aspects of thesis	Clear thesis & purpose, but too broad or unfocused	Thesis is unclear, unsupportable, vague or confusing; purpose is unclear
CONTENT	Good background info; comprehensive approach; excellent insight into topic; evidence of strong reflective analysis and keen awareness of audience	Satisfactory background info; comprehensive approach; good insight into topic; evidence of good reflective analysis and general awareness of audience	Some background info, but offers only routine or general insight into topic; evidence of some reflective analysis; may have a few inconsistencies in addressing audience and purpose	Too much or too little info; may be too specialized or personal for general audience; evidence of weak reflective analysis; inconsistencies detract from text's overall development
SUPPORT	Excellent support drawn from student's experience and knowledge; examples work to enhance and deepen the focus of the thesis	Good support drawn from student's experience and knowledge; examples work to illustrate the focus of the thesis	Support comes primarily from either student's experience or knowledge; examples work only minimally to support the focus of the thesis	Support may be irrelevant or unsubstantiated; examples may contradict or offer little support for the focus of the thesis
ORGANIZATION & STRUCTURE	Clear, logical progression of ideas; argument builds in strength; paper contains clear, engaging introduction that previews the paper's main argument; paper has coherent, well-developed paragraphs and uses transitional phrases effectively; paper also contains strong conclusion, which draws together and summarizes main points	Clear, logical progression of ideas, although some parts of argument may be stronger and more developed than others; good use of paragraphs to develop and organize main points; uses a number of transitional phrases to signal shifts and connections; paper contains clearly defined introduction and conclusion	Halting progression of ideas; some parts of argument may be weak or out of balance with others; a few undeveloped paragraphs and phrases; paper contains an introduction and conclusion, but they may be weak or generalized	Paragraphs seem out of order; argument is undeveloped and paragraphs may be lacking clear transitions or connections between each other; introduction and conclusion may be missing or lack connection to the rest of the paper

(continued)

	EXCELLENT	GOOD	FAIR	WEAK
WRITTEN QUALITY	Uses college-level vocabulary; varies sentences and wording; uses vivid examples; has strong, consistent voice and appears fluent in nature	Uses college-level vocabulary; varies sentences and wording; uses good examples but may fluctuate in tone or voice or fluency	Uneven quality of writing; relies heavily on two or three types of sentences; redundant in places; choppy or halting voice	Unclear, unvaried sentences; suffers from wordiness, slang or under-developed thoughts; distracting gestures; lists examples, rather than combining for complex sentences
MECHANICS	Excellent grammar, spelling, usage, and punctuation; paper flows effortlessly and reads well	Good use of grammar and mechanics; no more than 5–7 errors per page; paper flows well	Fair use of grammar and mechanics; errors are mostly minor in nature; paper is readable despite some distractions	Frequent or consistent errors in grammar and mechanics; interferes substantially with readability of paper

Expectations and Grading for Oral Presentations

	EXCELLENT	GOOD	FAIR	WEAK
ORGANIZATION	Presents information in well-organized, interesting manner; focuses on a central idea or narrowed aspect of his/her research; speech flows well, building to strong conclusion	Presents information in well-organized, interesting manner, but may try to cover too much or too little of his/her research; speech flows well, building to conclusion	Presents information in an interesting but general manner; focuses on more than one aspect of research; speaker may digress from thesis and have difficulty getting back	Presents information in a random and vague manner; unclear transitions between parts; focuses on broad topic, not central thesis or narrowed aspect; speech appears unrehearsed
ACTIVE INVOLVEMENT	Actively involves the class through use of props, learning exercises, handouts, and other techniques; creatively teaches an aspect of the research	Involves the class through use of props or other aids, and attempts to engage the audience in his/her research, although primarily as listeners, not doers	Involves the audience through use of some visual aids, but may not explain nor use them in effective ways may read or recite excerpts from paper	Does not include the audience in the presentation; reads from whole paper or extended parts of paper; does not provide good supplementary material for audience
CONTENT	Demonstrates superb knowledge & understanding of topic; supports ideas with vivid examples & details; makes relevant connections for others	Demonstrates good knowledge & understanding of topic; supports ideas with clear, factual data; makes some connections	Demonstrates fair knowledge & understanding of the topic, but may have difficulty explaining certain aspects of the topic or relating knowledge to other areas of thought	Demonstrates minimal knowledge & understanding of the topic; has problems supporting his/her main point, and may offer contradictory or confusing examples
VOICE	Demonstrates great enthusiasm for topic; speaks clearly and loudly enough to be understood easily; varies tone and pitch for animated speaking style	Demonstrates comfort in speaking; speaks clearly and with emphasis; may illustrate a bit of nervousness and/or shaky voice at the beginning	Demonstrates some nervousness or discomfort at speaking, but uses appropriate pace, tone and volume to be heard clearly for much of the time	May appear nervous or troubled, voice too quiet or monotone to be heard effectively; may rush through his/her sentences or speak in halting, slow manner
BODY LANGUAGE	Makes effective eye contact with whole audience throughout the presentation; uses gestures and body language to emphasize certain points	Makes good eye contact but limits it to only a few people; is expressive in his/her gestures although they may be unrelated to key points	Makes some eye contact, but not for duration and not with more than a couple of people; may look stiff or uncomfortable while presenting	Fidgets or engages in other nervous movements; makes little or no eye contact; uses ineffective or distracting gestures

Expectations and Grading for Research Papers

	EXCELLENT	GOOD	FAIR	WEAK
FOCUS **Points 1–15** Score_____	Clear, central thesis and purpose; paper addresses all aspects of thesis	Clear, central thesis and purpose; paper addresses some aspects of thesis	Clear thesis and purpose, but too broad or unfocused	Thesis is unclear, unsupportable, vague or confusing. Purpose is difficult to identify.
CONTENT **Points 1–15** Score_____	Good background info.; comprehensive approach; excellent insight into topic	Enough background info.; comprehensive approach; good insight into topic	Some background info., but offers only routine or general insight into topic	Too much or too little info.; may be too specialized or general for serious college reader
SUPPORT **Points 1–15** Score_____	Excellent support selected from wide variety of appropriate sources; support blends well with writer's own words	Good support selected from a variety of appropriate sources; uses direct quotes sparingly	Support comes mostly from 2–3 sources; paper uses some direct quotes when paraphrasing would be better	Support is biased, irrelevant, or contained to 1–2 major sources; paper uses many long quotes that are not well integrated
ORGANIZATION & STRUCTURE **Points 1–15** Score_____	Clear, logical progression of ideas, argument builds in strength, coherent paragraphs consisting of 7–11 sentences	Clear, logical progression of ideas although some parts of argument may be stronger and more developed; good use of paragraphs	Halting progression of ideas; some parts of argument may be weak or out of balance with others; some undeveloped paragraphs	Paragraphs seem out of order or non-exisitent; argument is undeveloped and lacking clear transitions from one part to another
WRITTEN QUALITY **Points 1–10** Score_____	Uses college-level vocabulary; varies sentences and wording; uses vivid examples; has strong, consistent voice	Uses college-level vocabulary; varies sentences and wording; uses good examples, but may fluctuate in tone or voice	Uneven quality in the writing; relies heavily on 2–3 types of sentences; redundant in a few places; choppy or halting voice	Unclear, unvaried sentences; suffers from wordiness, slang, or underdeveloped thoughts; lists examples rather than combining for complex sentences
MECHANICS **Points 1–10** Score_____	Excellent grammar, spelling, usage, and punctuation; paper flows well and reads easily	Good use of grammar and mechanics; no more than 3-4 errors per page; paper flows well	Fair use of mechanics; some errors but minor in nature; paper is readable despite some distraction	Frequent or consistent errors in grammar and mechanics; interferes with readability of paper
RESEARCH FORMAT **Points 1–20** Score_____	Uses proper MLA format; cites sources correctly within body of the paper, and uses correct format for Works Cited; clearly gives credit for others' ideas	Uses proper MLA format most of the time; cites sources correctly, although there may be minor errors in format punctuation or rules; clearly gives credit for others' ideas	Has some problems in consistency of format; citations may show problems with punctuation or format, but still relatively minor in nature; clearly gives credit for others' ideas	Major problems in format; does not demonstrate proper MLA citation of sources; may plagiarize* and/or misrepresent sources; confuses own ideas with those from sources

TOTAL SCORE/GRADE: _____ *Plagiarism may result in a ZERO for this assignment and the course.*

This matrix (Werner, 2000) is a conceptual device to be used when designing a course. It is critical to determine how our learning objectives connect to other elements of planning, such as class activities, student assessment, evaluation methods, and resources. Thinking about how to teach while accommodating a wide variety of learning styles and reflecting on the pace and sequence of learning can also be important in establishing an effective climate for learning.

Matrix for Course Planning				
Essential Objectives	Topic Content	Sequence Dates	Reading & Assignments	In-Class Activities
Learning Styles	Teacher Demonstrations	Informal Assessments	Evaluation	Resources

Note: Adapted from Werner (2000) by permission.

Reflective Checklist for Teaching

I HAVE...	YES	NOT YET
Thought about how to keep my students involved and challenged		
Prepared for dealing with dissonance in the classroom		
Prepared course materials so that students may connect their knowledge to real-life experiences		
Prepared hooks that tie the content into a bigger picture that students can understand		
Developed an ongoing class project that ties together course content throughout the semester and is designed to maintain students' interest		
Surveyed or thought about the spatial arrangements of the classroom in order to optimize the use of furniture and promote community; surveyed or thought about the spatial and visual arrangements of my online classroom to promote clarity and community		
Developed class activities that will allow students to investigate and reorganize content in creative and personally relevant ways		
Integrated opportunities for students to write critically and reflectively in the classroom and in assignments		
Developed a forum where students have the ability to reflect in an open-minded way on what does and does not make sense regarding the materials they are learning; developed opportunities for students to reflect on their own performance in class		
Prepared a syllabus and lesson plan that address the essential learning objectives of the course with a variety of teaching methods		
Thought about the different learning styles that may be present in the class or in me, and have prepared activities that will address student diversity		
Thought about what the key questions or concepts are in my course and have emphasized these in various ways		

Programs for faculty orientation and development exist at most colleges. Community College of Vermont has designed an orientation for all instructors who are new to teaching at the college. Great Beginnings introduces topics such as active learning, diversity, and evaluation; it also models teaching in the seminar format. The orientation begins with a reflective exercise that allows instructors to think about their own educational experience— who they are as learners and who they want to be as teachers. Because we all can benefit from reflecting on our goals, no matter how long we have taught, the following exercise merits reading:

- Think of a teacher who has had a profoundly positive impact on your life. Envision this teacher and think about the behaviors that he or she used in the classroom and with students.

- Take a few moments to write your impressions, memories, and thoughts about the teacher you have in mind.

- After a few minutes of writing, consult the checklist titled "Effective Teaching Characteristics Checklist."

- Make an X next to the characteristics exemplified by your teacher.

- Now make a leap from the teacher you have in mind to college teachers in general. Which of the characteristics on the checklist are most important? What are the five most important things teachers have to be or do in the college classroom?

- Is there any relationship between the characteristics embodied by your teacher and those you believe are important? How did you choose among the characteristics, and how do these choices reflect your values and priorities?

This exercise reminds us why we teach. It encourages us to locate the image of teacher in our minds and analyze it for effective behavior or characteristics. In the process, we can confront our assumptions about teaching and learning. When Palmer (1997) asserted that good teaching emerges from both the identity and integrity of the instructor, he reminds us that this is not just an exercise in determining our goodness; "identity and integrity have as much to do with our shadows and limits, our wounds and fears, as with our strength and potentials" (p. 13). By reflecting on our experiences and memories, we can explore the various selves we carry with us to each class.

Think of a teacher who had a profoundly positive influence on you as a student. This could be a teacher from elementary school or high school or a professor from your postsecondary experience. From the following list, decide which characteristics your teacher exemplified and mark an X next to them.

My Teacher…

___liked or was interested in students

___was organized and clear about expectations

___encouraged independence through showing students how to learn

___demonstrated love of subject and was enthusiastic

___was flexible and willing to change under certain circumstances

___was compassionate and encouraging

___made the material meaningful and relevant to students

___was fun-loving and humorous

___was knowledgeable about the subject

___valued students' ideas and was a good listener

___taught problem-solving through encouraging students to think for themselves

___was expressive, conveyed genuine affection for all students

___was fair to all students, demonstrated integrity

___demonstrated excellent speaking skills and was able to keep students' attention

___was consistent in how he or she presented expectations and requirements

___inspired and/or challenged students

___was friendly and personable

___was energetic and dynamic

Student Feedback Form

COURSE TITLE_____ DATE_____

INSTRUCTOR'S NAME_____ SEMESTER_____

Number of Courses Taken _____
Level of Education: ☐ High School ☐ Some College ☐ A.D. ☐ B.A. ☐ M.A. ☐ Ph.D.

YOUR HONEST AND OBJECTIVE RESPONSES WILL HELP CCV IMPROVE INSTRUCTION AND ADDRESS YOUR NEEDS AS A STUDENT.
PLEASE EVALUATE THE INSTRUCTION YOU RECEIVED BY CHECKING THE APPROPRIATE BOXES BELOW.

1. Good instructors foster a respectful classroom environment.

	STRONGLY AGREE	AGREE	NEUTRAL	DISAGREE	STRONGLY DISAGREE
Treated students in a positive and respectful manner	☐	☐	☐	☐	☐
Made good use of class time	☐	☐	☐	☐	☐
Responded to students' needs and provided feedback on their academic progress	☐	☐	☐	☐	☐
Was fair and approachable to all students	☐	☐	☐	☐	☐
Was reasonably available to students	☐	☐	☐	☐	☐

Additional Comments:

2. Good instructors are motivated and, in turn, motivate others.

	STRONGLY AGREE	AGREE	NEUTRAL	DISAGREE	STRONGLY DISAGREE
Set challenging goals for students	☐	☐	☐	☐	☐
Demonstrated enthusiasm for learning	☐	☐	☐	☐	☐
Demonstrated enthusiasm for the subject he/she was teaching	☐	☐	☐	☐	☐
Helped students to become effective learners	☐	☐	☐	☐	☐

Additional Comments:

3. Good instructors create a classroom environment that is dynamic and connected.

	STRONGLY AGREE	AGREE	NEUTRAL	DISAGREE	STRONGLY DISAGREE
Provided opportunities for hands-on learning	☐	☐	☐	☐	☐
Provided opportunities for students to reflect on their learning in a meaningful way	☐	☐	☐	☐	☐
Made connections between classroom content and the world at large	☐	☐	☐	☐	☐

Additional Comments:

4. Good instructors share their knowledge with students in a contextual, organized and relevant manner.

	STRONGLY AGREE	AGREE	NEUTRAL	DISAGREE	STRONGLY DISAGREE
Demonstrated strong knowledge of the subject	☐	☐	☐	☐	☐
Presented activities for different types of learners	☐	☐	☐	☐	☐
Was well-prepared and organized	☐	☐	☐	☐	☐
Clearly articulated his/her expectations	☐	☐	☐	☐	☐
Made good use of materials or textbooks	☐	☐	☐	☐	☐

Additional Comments:

5. **Good instructors encourage collaboration and dialogue.**

	Strongly Agree	Agree	Neutral	Disagree	Strongly Disagree
Promoted student-to-student dialogue through the use of small groups	☐	☐	☐	☐	☐
Generated effective discussions and questions_ _ _ _ _ _ _ _ _ _ _ _ _ _	☐	☐	☐	☐	☐
Encouraged students to share their knowledge and skills with each other	☐	☐	☐	☐	☐

Additional Comments:

6. **Good instructors provide opportunities for active learning.**

	Strongly Agree	Agree	Neutral	Disagree	Strongly Disagree
Created opportunities for students to actively apply their knowledge and skills _	☐	☐	☐	☐	☐
Developed assignments that promoted critical thinking and research _	☐	☐	☐	☐	☐
Developed activities that encouraged students to problem-solve and take risks in their learning _	☐	☐	☐	☐	☐

Additional Comments:

7. **Good instructors help students to develop as learners.**

	Strongly Agree	Agree	Neutral	Disagree	Strongly Disagree
Created an environment of safety and trust in the classroom_ _ _ _ _ _	☐	☐	☐	☐	☐
Provided opportunities for students to examine their thoughts, values, and assumptions _	☐	☐	☐	☐	☐
Developed activities that were challenging but not frustrating to students	☐	☐	☐	☐	☐

Additional Comments:

8. **Good instructors provide ongoing assessment to learners.**

	Strongly Agree	Agree	Neutral	Disagree	Strongly Disagree
Assessed students in a way that helped them grow as learners_ _ _ _ _	☐	☐	☐	☐	☐
Connected tests, assignments and other material to the content and objectives of the course_ _	☐	☐	☐	☐	☐
Demonstrated the process of giving and receiving appropriate feedback	☐	☐	☐	☐	☐

Additional Comments:

9. **Additional comments you have regarding the course (e.g., amount of homework, comments about texts or materials used, etc.):**

Useful Sources for Teaching and Learning

Web Sites

American Association of Community Colleges
http://www.aacc.nche.edu

American Community College Education
http://www.americancommunitycolleges.com

Berkeley Compendium of Suggestions for Teaching with Excellence
http://teaching.berkeley.edu/compendium

Center for Teaching at the University of Iowa: Teaching Goals Inventory
http://www.uiowa.edu/~centeach/tgi

Community College Journal and *Community College Times* archives
http://www.aaccarchives.org

Community College Week
http://www.ccweek.com

Foundation for Critical Thinking: Faculty Resources
http://www.criticalthinking.org/University/univclass/trc.html

Honolulu Community College's Teaching Tips Index
http://honolulu.hawaii.edu/intranet/committees/FacDevCom/guidebk/teachtip/teachtip.htm

Iowa State University's Center for Teaching Excellence
http://www.cte.iastate.edu/tips

League for Innovation in the Community College
http://www.league.org/welcome.htm

Maricopa Community Colleges' Center for Learning & Instruction
http://www.mcli.dist.maricopa.edu

National Teaching & Learning Forum
http://www.ntlf.com

Penn State's National Center for Post Secondary Teaching, Learning, and Assessment
ttp://www.ed.psu.edu/cshe/nctla.html

Purdue University's Online Writing Lab
http://owl.english.purdue.edu

Journals and Newsletters

College Teaching
A cross-disciplinary journal published quarterly. Heldref Publications.

The Journal on Excellence in College Teaching
A peer-reviewed journal published at the University of Miami three times a year.

The National Teaching and Learning Forum
A newsletter/journal published six times each year. James Rhem and Associates.

The Teaching Professor
A monthly newsletter/journal, Magna Publications.

Deborah A. Stewart is associate academic dean at the Community College of Vermont. After graduating from the college in 1989, she went on to pursue an education in writing and literature, earning an MFA in writing from Vermont College in 1993. She has published poems and reviews in the *Harvard Review*, *Sojourner*, *Poet Lore*, and other journals. She has been a finalist for the Academy of American Poets' Walt Whitman Award (1994), runner-up for Kent State's Wick Poetry Prize (1994), semifinalist for University of Wisconsin's Brittingham Award (1995), and semifinalist for the National Poetry Series (1997, 1998). She has performed her poetry in Vermont and New Hampshire as part of the Councils on the Humanities' "After Frost" program (1995–1997).

Stewart began teaching at the Community College of Vermont in 1993. She has taught writing, literature, humanities, communication, and education courses. She also served as an academic coordinator at CCV before taking a position in the dean's office. In her current capacity, Stewart works closely on issues of instructor development; she chairs the writing, communication, and humanities committee; and she continues to teach, online and on-ground, nearly every semester. In 2003 Stewart graduated from the Snelling Center for Government's Vermont Leadership Institute.

NOTES

NOTES